W9-CWO-232

WHAT ARE YOU WORTH?

BOOKS BY

Graef S. Crystal

◆

Financial Motivation for Executives

Executive Compensation

*Questions and Answers
on Executive Compensation*

In Search of Excess

the chief executive press

WHAT ARE YOU WORTH?

GRAEF S. CRYSTAL

whittle direct books

Copyright ©1992 by Graef S. Crystal

All rights reserved, including the right of reproduction
in whole or in part, in any form.

Photographs: Michael Eisner, David Strick/Onyx, page 10; Kenneth H.
Olsen, John S. Abbott, page 25; Joseph D. Williams, Rob Kinmonth,
page 63; Burton J. Manning, John S. Abbott, page 70
Charts: Linda Eckstein

Library of Congress Catalog Card Number: 92-81407
Crystal, Graef S.
What Are You Worth?
ISBN 1-879736-07-1
ISSN 1060-8923

the chief executive press

The Chief Executive Press presents original short books by distinguished authors on subjects of special importance to the topmost executives of the world's major businesses.

The series is edited and published by Whittle Books, a business unit of Whittle Communications L.P. Books will appear several times a year, and the series will reflect a broad spectrum of responsible opinions. In each book the opinions expressed are those of the author, not the publisher or the advertiser.

I welcome your comments on this ambitious endeavor.

William S. Rukeyser
Editor in Chief

For Sue—
for everything.

ACKNOWLEDGMENTS

In preparing to write this book, I sought to interview a number of CEOs who I knew could offer me some guidance. Several of those I contacted chose not to talk with me, perhaps because of my reputation as a critic of executive pay. But eight CEOs did agree to talk, and I am most indebted to each of them. They include Michael Eisner of Walt Disney, Burton J. Manning of J. Walter Thompson, Edmund T. Pratt Jr., the retired CEO of Pfizer Inc., John S. Reed of Citicorp, Russell S. Reynolds Jr. of Russell Reynolds Associates, Gerard R. Roche of Heidrick & Struggles, Dan Tellep of Lockheed Corporation, and Joseph D. Williams, the retired CEO of Warner-Lambert Company. I also benefited from listening to a speech given by George M. Keller, the retired CEO of Chevron, at a University of California seminar I organized.

These current and former CEOs gave to me not only of their time but of their wisdom. They forced me to understand that, although I am supposedly the expert, I do not have all the answers. My heartfelt thanks to each of them.

CONTENTS

FOREWORD

When you as a CEO recommend to your board of directors that the company's R&D budget be increased, or that a new plant be built, or that a division be sold off, everyone presumes that you have the best interests of the business at heart and that you are in no way motivated by personal considerations. But one set of recommendations that you make cannot, by definition, be conflict-free: those regarding the pay of your key executive subordinates and, by extension, your own pay. For you are acting not only as the CEO and as a fiduciary for your shareholders but also as an agent for yourself. To be sure, you may not be suggesting to your board that you be paid a bonus of $650,000, but if you are recommending that your chief financial officer be given a bonus of $250,000 and that your chief operating officer be given one of $400,000, well, your board can extrapolate as skillfully as the next.

As you must know better than almost anyone else, a great national debate is flaring over how *much* you are paid and also over *how* you are paid. Through the long recession, the media have had a picnic pointing out how much you are compensated in relation to workers in your companies, as well as to your counterparts in Japan and Germany, and how executive pay seems to float free of any considerations of company performance.

Some companies are already responding. In the face of depressed profits and severe criticism of their compensation policies, IBM, ITT, and American Express have recently made no-fooling cuts in their CEOs' pay packages. In some other major companies-—Sears, Roebuck; Browning-Ferris; UAL, the parent of United Air Lines; AMR, the parent of American Airlines; FCB Communications—CEOs have relinquished annual bonuses and have had their other incentive plans linked more tightly to the performance of the companies' stock. Even the Japanese are getting into the act. Although their pay levels are already comparatively low, and few chief executives receive raises just because performance is good, some Japanese CEOs are nonetheless adjusting their pay to match lower company performance.

In this climate, every company needs to examine critically its executive compensation levels and the sensitivity of those levels to company performance. Because if you and your company don't take on this task, it's likely others will.

Michigan senator Carl Levin has sponsored federal legislation designed to provide institutional shareholders more weapons in their battle to lower your pay. Minnesota congressman Martin Sabo wants to deny your company its tax deduction for any part of your pay that is higher than 25 times the pay of your lowest-paid workers—roughly the same ratio as the one between President Bush's salary and the minimum wage. And various other Democratic senators and representatives are warming up in the bullpen of taxation. They cannot fail to note that in this country the maximum marginal federal tax rate, now 31 percent, was as high as 91 percent before 1964. The maximum marginal rates in Japan and Germany are near 60 percent.

Those who want to cut your pay are in two philosophical camps. On the one hand are the "interventionists," who would be quite happy to see Congress act vigorously. Indeed, the interventionists wouldn't mind an outright pay freeze like the one that President Nixon introduced as recently as 1973.

The other camp can be described as the "free marketeers." They abhor the intrusion of more government regulations. They endorse the concept of free markets and accept that an executive's pay is merely the price of his labor. But they do not accept that a free market is operating today for CEO pay. For a price to be fair, they argue, vigorous arm's-length bargaining must occur between informed buyers and informed sellers. They can readily see how the CEO is an informed seller of his talent, because, among other things, he is flanked by his personnel staff and his outside compensation consultant. But they cannot see how the board of directors or its compensation committee can be informed buyers of talent because its members spend little time analyzing the complex issues and, more important, because they are not given expert help. Moreover, the free marketeers note, the CEO usually plays a major role in determining who gets elected to board membership, thereby assuring that the buyers of talent are likely to be well disposed to the seller: in an almost endless loop, the CEO reports to the board, and the board reports to the CEO, since he is after all the chairman of the board. This power balance, however, is changing. Witness the action recently taken by General Motors' board when it demoted two key executives and reduced the power of the CEO.

Finally, free marketeers observe that almost none of the variation in senior executive pay can be traced to differences in corporate performance. A free market is, by definition, rational, so a market that allocates the vast majority of its resources (read "pay levels") on considerations other than company size and performance can hardly be considered a free market. The result, they claim, is pay that is disproportionately higher than the value of the corporate performance.

The solution is to force changes that will create a free market. The free marketeers would strengthen the role of the compensation committee by ensuring that its members are conflict-free and by providing the committee with its own outside consultant—a consultant with no economic ties to the management of the company. They would also push the government to require more comprehensive proxy disclosure of executive pay and the Financial Accounting Standards Board to force companies to charge their earnings with the present value of stock-option grants. Finally, the most ardent free marketeers would shove the CEO and other inside directors off the board and elect a nonsupervisory chairman.

I am in the free-marketeer camp. I want to help create a truly free market for executive talent. And I am willing to accept whatever pay levels result. Most important, I want to see companies pay for performance and not merely give the concept lip service, as many have in recent years. Perhaps, as professors Michael Jensen and Kevin Murphy of the Harvard Business School argue, the quid pro quo for more pay-for-performance among CEOs will be still higher compensation. If that occurs through the operation of a truly free market, then so be it.

As you likely know, I have become the most vocal critic of senior executive pay. Before that, I was generally considered the top consultant in the area. Various motives have been attributed to my behavioral sea change, none flattering. They range from a desire to hype the sales of my previous book, *In Search of Excess*, to having a traitorous streak to breathing anew the communist-tainted air surrounding the University of California at Berkeley.

Looking back, I confess that I certainly helped create some of the pay abuse I now find. But I had a lot of help. And besides, I haven't been a compensation consultant for more than four years, and senior executive pay, far from dropping in the interval, has soared. Finally, if I hadn't begun shooting off my mouth, I could have made far more income as a compensation consultant than I now make teaching executive compensation and corporate governance courses at Berkeley, writing articles and columns for publications such as the *New York Observer* and *Pensions & Investments*, and editing my newsletter on executive compensation, *The Crystal Report*.

Although many CEOs have identified me as the proximate cause of their torment, I am merely the messenger. Shooting me is not going to make the problem go away. You also have to deal with other potential critics, including your shareholders, your employees, and the government. But if you are a high performer, that high performance can act as a sort of talisman with which you can hold your critics at bay. Michael Eisner of Walt Disney and Anthony J. F. O'Reilly of H. J. Heinz may well earn more than even their stellar performances merit. But both are willing to see their pay plummet in bad times and, far more important, both are brilliant performers.

If you are a poor performer, however, isn't it reasonable to assume that your performance has already generated smoldering resentment among your investors? So a viable strategy is *not* to continue to pay yourself a small fortune while hurling brickbats at your critics. Instead it makes more sense for you to cut your pay in line with your performance and to redesign your pay package so that if you turn your company around, you recoup all you have lost and then some.

Paying for performance, and so playing the pay game more fairly, carries a number of important advantages. For openers, it turns enemies, such as disgruntled employees and institutional shareholders, into friends. Second, it defangs skeptics in Congress. And third, it turns critics such as myself into fans.

Of those advantages, the first is by far the most important. If your employees perceive that in an economic downturn you are paying your dues—as they are—they may decide to work harder and smarter. Their greater productivity will in turn spur an even sharper upturn when the economy starts to grow again. And if your pay package has been well designed, that upturn will give you more economic rewards than a refusal to play the pay game fairly. Your shareholders may also be motivated to buy more shares and hold on to the shares they own. That in turn means higher stock prices. Once again, if your pay package has been designed right, you will be the beneficiary.

So playing the pay game fairly should not be viewed as the equivalent of going to church on Sunday—an uplifting experience that may possibly have some future payback. No, playing fair ought to give you a much more certain payback sooner.

In my last book I bashed a number of CEOs. In this book I will leave off bashing and offer instead my suggestions about how to play the pay game fairly and to your advantage. If that is your interest too, then please read on.

This is an exciting time for Cessna Aircraft. Throughout the year we have been observing "Citation Celebration 2000."

The first Citation business jet was delivered just 20 years ago, and we will be very proud to deliver the 2000th Citation in early 1993.

With substantially more Citations in service throughout the world than business jets of any other manufacturer, all of us at Cessna are deeply gratified by our market leadership.

But even more significant news remains on the horizon. Later this year we will make the first customer delivery of the all-new CitationJet. And mid-1993 will mark first flight of the Citation X, the fastest commercial aircraft in the world except for the Concorde.

As these two excellent new aircraft join our current lineup of Citation II, Citation V, Citation VI and Citation VII models, we're strongly positioned to provide an even broader range of business jets throughout this decade and into the next century.

Sincerely yours,

Russell W. Meyer, Jr.
Chairman and Chief Executive Officer
Cessna Aircraft Company

Cessna Aircraft Company · One Cessna Boulevard · Wichita, Kansas 67212 · 316/941-7400

Cessna
A Textron Company

Chapter One

Executive Pay Packages: Riskier Is Better

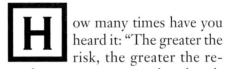ow many times have you heard it: "The greater the risk, the greater the reward"? Stocks deliver greater long-term returns than bonds because their prices fluctuate so much more. And risky stocks deliver greater long-term returns than less risky stocks.

Risk, in this case, means volatility or uncertainty of outcome. And this uncertainty is what distinguishes a risky pay package from one that contains little hazard. In short, the hallmark of a risky pay package is variability.

Now, variability in stock returns has at least some random components. Put another way, good guys don't always finish first—at least in the short run. But variability in CEO pay packages is not intended to be random. Rather, variability should conform to variability in company performance, especially in the long term.

Let's face it, if you want to earn a ton of money, sleep well, and avoid picking up a magazine that has your face and compensation splashed over the cover, you're going to have to accept a lot more variability in your pay package than you've probably been accustomed to. Or you're going to have to take drastic pay cuts that bring your income in line with your reduced risk. The song about love and marriage says you can't have one without the other. The song about reward and risk says the same thing.

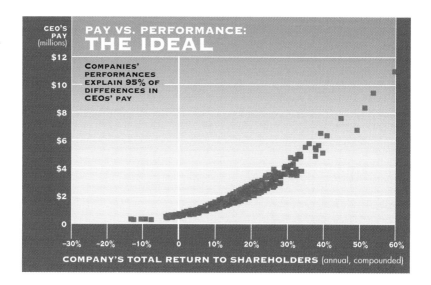

This cometlike curve is how compensation would look if companies' long-term performance (measured by a weighted 10-year return to shareholders) truly determined the pay of CEOs. Each square represents the compensation of the CEO of one of the 500 largest U.S. corporations, measured by stock-market value. The highest-paid CEOs are found at the right, where the shareholders are also getting wealthy.

◆

But while you're concentrating on the hit that your pocketbook is going to take in bad times, don't neglect the much more appealing outcomes that can occur in good times. For adding more risk to your pay package is also likely to produce more reward if you perform above average for a long time.

Among the CEOs I interviewed, opinion is unanimous that senior executive pay packages must contain a good deal of risk. George M. Keller, the retired CEO of Chevron, has observed: "Today a typical corporate compensation structure looks like a pyramid with the Eiffel Tower sticking out the top." Keller is not necessarily attacking the Eiffel Tower of compensation itself, only that it seems to stand up no matter what the level of corporate performance. Observing the reluctance to cut pay in bad times, Citicorp's John S. Reed, who has experienced low points during his tenure as CEO, said: "Senior executives simply have to bear the brunt of reality in their pay packages."

But although every CEO I interviewed favors a high degree of

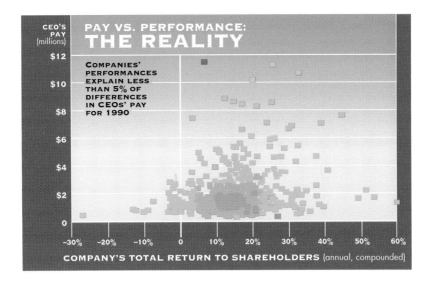

This hornet's nest shows how the compensation of those 500 chief executives in 1990 actually related to shareholders' long-term gains. (A few extreme cases have been omitted to avoid distortion.) Notice that, among other things, the lowest-paid CEO on the chart (green square) led a company whose performance was distinctly better than the company with the highest-paid CEO (red square).

◆

pay risk in return for a high degree of pay reward, the records reveal a different picture. In 1991 I looked at the 1990 pay of CEOs of the 500 companies with the highest equity capitalization (the market value of their outstanding shares). In calculating pay, I included not only the CEO's base salary and bonus but also the present value of stock-option grants and the value of restricted-stock and performance-share and performance-unit awards. Ignoring some statistical outliers, the total compensation ranged from $250,000 to $11.5 million.

Now, if the market for CEO talent were efficient and rational, some of that variance would result from differing company size, but most would be accounted for by differing company performance. The chart on the facing page shows how the market might look if CEO pay were truly driven by total shareholder returns (a weighted average of returns, including stock-price appreciation and reinvested dividends, for one year, two years, and so forth through 10 years). Contrast this with the chart above, which shows the *actual* relationship of CEO pay to weighted average total share-holder returns. As you can see, less than 5 percent of the variance can be laid at the door of company performance. This chart, more than any other you might look at, indicates the extent to which the market for CEO talent deviates from a free market. The almost random scattering of squares triggers two fundamental questions. First, why would any shareholder who is not ingesting a controlled substance want to pay someone $11.5 million per year, if not for brilliant performance? And why would any big-company CEO who is not the world's worst performer want to work for $250,000 per year?

The median income among the 500 CEOs studied is $2 million per year. If hardly any relationship between CEO pay and company performance exists, then whenever the U.S. economy turns down, as it recently has, CEO pay will not decrease correspondingly. That is why this issue is currently such a burning one.

It's long been debatable whether the threat of capital punishment alters behavior. It's just as debatable whether the size of the pay package alters CEO performance. "It's hard to see how money is really motivating me these days," said Dan Tellep, Lockheed's CEO. "I'm working as flat-out as I can." Citicorp's Reed said, "I don't measure the value of my life by how much I make." And Walt Disney's Michael Eisner told me, "I would have worked just as hard if I had been paid less." But Burton J. Manning, the CEO of one of America's largest advertising agencies, J. Walter Thompson, said, "The possibility of earning more money can change the behavior of even a highly paid person, provided that he believes he can affect the outcome."

Even if your typical CEO won't admit to working harder or smarter for more money, the bloodlust argument remains: shareholders as well as the public need to see CEO pay plummet in bad times. Yet if that is to happen, CEO pay must of necessity soar in good times, whether or not the possibility of more pay motivates greater or smarter performance. Indeed, the possibility of high rewards in good times represents one of the most potent ways of keeping people in bad times. As Burt Manning put it: "When an entire industry, like advertising, is in the dumps, it really isn't hard to keep good people. After all, where are they going to go? But if you aren't willing to really pay for performance when times are good, then when times finally do improve, you lose all your best people." Echoing Manning, Eisner said: "If you're going to reward heavily for success, you shouldn't have to overpay in poor times."

"If you're going to reward heavily for success, you shouldn't have to overpay in poor times."

Michael Eisner
Chief Executive Officer
Walt Disney

Neither Manning nor Eisner is adopting the all-too-familiar argument that you have to pay good people a lot of money even in bad times or they will depart for greener pastures. And neither is arguing for tying up huge amounts of the executive's money so that he would lose heavily by quitting. No, they are pushing a different notion: that executives have good memories and a decent sense of fairness. If they believe that excellent performance will be well rewarded, they are apt to slog through bad times with an admixture of stoicism and expectations for the good times. As Eisner said: "The best way to hold talent in the bad years is to really lay it on heavy in the good years."

Consider the behavior of Lee Iacocca when he joined Chrysler in 1978. He offered to work for $1 per year in exchange for a huge number of stock-option shares. He was so successful, at least in his early years, that he received more than $40 million in option profits. No one begrudged him his millions at the time, because everyone understood the risk he had taken. You don't need to go as far as Iacocca, but you do need to head in that direction.

Injecting more risk into your pay package will not only help you with your shareholders, your workers, and the government, it will also provide the philosophical defense you need for earning more than your counterparts in Japan and Germany. For although Japanese and German CEOs earn only a pittance compared to you, they also take much less pay risk. Their total compensation packages consist mainly of base salary, as well as—until very recently, at least—a relatively unvarying annual bonus. So Japanese and German CEOs have deserved relatively low compensation. As Citicorp's Reed put it: "Overseas CEOs are more buffered on the downside. They should, by rights, receive less pay on the upside."

You must, in short, find ways to inject a lot more risk into your pay package. But as already noted, injecting more risk hurts only when performance is poor. If you perform well, risk can be an altogether pleasant experience, as you reap the greater rewards that accompany the greater gamble.

THE U.S. LEADER
ELECTED BY THE ENTIRE WORLD.

Of all the business jet choices today, one line is the undisputed leader. One is chosen by more companies than any other.

Before choosing, most companies carefully evaluated several candidates. They looked at overall performance and operating cost. They compared safety records. Reliability. Cabin comfort. And support networks.

Then companies in 49 U.S. states and in 58 other nations all arrived at the same sensible conclusion. They all bought Cessna Citations.

THE SENSIBLE CITATIONS

Cessna
A Textron Company

COMPARATOR GROUPS AND PAY SURVEYS

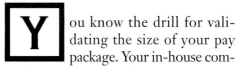ou know the drill for validating the size of your pay package. Your in-house compensation group or your outside consultant conducts a survey, you present the results to your compensation committee, and then, assuming the survey shows that your pay is below average, you sit back and wait for the money to roll in.

Nothing is inherently wrong with this process, but it can be greatly improved if you are willing to spend a bit of your personal time on it. And one area that can clearly benefit from your wisdom is the selection of the companies composing the so-called comparator group.

In choosing a particular company, your consultant usually considers its size, industry status, and sometimes, location. If yours is a $2 billion food company headquartered in Dallas, ideally the consultant would form a comparator group consisting of Dallas-based food companies in the $1 billion to $3 billion range. But he may well find that the group consists of only one company: yours. As an alternative he might survey companies in the $1 billion to $3 billion range, regardless of industry. Or he might survey food companies more or less regardless of size. Or he might survey companies in Dallas, again regardless of size. Whatever the decision, you will not likely be asked to approve the final list or, if asked, you will give the list only the most cursory examination.

That's a pity, because the selection of comparator companies can have a huge influence on the survey results. Perhaps the consultant will select a particular company because he believes it to be in the food industry. But had you seen the selection, you would have rejected it, because you know the company is rapidly diversifying into other industries. Or perhaps the consultant has, wittingly or unwittingly, included a company whose CEO earns a ton of money. To be sure, the inclusion of this company will raise the survey averages, but is the inclusion fair to your trusting board and shareholders?

If survey results are to be believed and accepted, the list of companies must meet what I call a smell test. In effect, given the list, a knowledgeable observer ought to comprehend instantly the reason any particular company is included and conclude that on balance the list is representative. For the companies are a sample and not a universe. As such, the list needs to be representative of the broader universe or the results will be skewed. Among other things, this means that certain CEOs ought not to be included in any comparator group because their pay is so high it will skew the averages and challenge the validity of the survey. You know who those CEOs are.

In selecting your comparator group, act as though the companies' names are going to be published in your proxy statement. If any company doesn't smell right, don't consider it. Indeed, why not go as far as Vulcan Materials Company, whose board actually published the company's list of comparator companies in its proxy statement? That way your shareholders will have a better understanding of why you're paid what you are.

You should also consider including some of your key foreign competitors. When General Motors conducts a compensation survey, Ford and Chrysler are surely among its comparator companies. But how about Toyota and Nissan? Many auto-industry analysts believe these Japanese companies are far more formidable competitors for GM than Ford and Chrysler. Of course, the inclusion of overseas companies will very likely reduce the resulting averages. So be it. Restricting a survey comparator group to American companies is anachronistic. Like as not, your principal competitors these days are headquartered overseas. (But is their inclusion fair, you ask, since the Japanese inject at least somewhat less risk in their pay packages? Yes, because that's also true of some American companies that pay a great deal more than the Japanese.)

Selecting the right group of comparator companies—besides validating your fundamental sense of fairness—carries two other potential advantages. First, it reassures your board that your primary goal is to do what's right, not what lines your pockets. That reassurance can pay big dividends the next time you ask your board to go along with a bold strategic move. And second, selecting the right comparator companies may help you concentrate not merely on the cost of your labor but on the labor cost of all your employees. For if including Japanese and German companies in the group is fair, then is it not equally fair to include those companies in the group used to set the pay of your factory workers? If this reasoning leads to reduced labor costs, not only for you but for other employees, then so be it. The result will be a leaner, meaner corporation that one day may emerge as a world-class competitor. When that happens, you and your employees can rightfully be rewarded for your earlier fair decision-making.

Once you have chosen the comparator group, you need to choose the forms of compensation to survey. Here the watchword is comprehensiveness. It makes little sense to survey base salaries and annual bonuses without also looking at the various forms of long-term incentive compensation such as stock-option grants, restricted-stock awards, and performance-share and performance-unit payouts. Moreover, you need to pay attention to perquisites, broad-based employee fringe benefits, and supplemental executive benefits if your company is doing anything unusual in these areas. I wouldn't be concerned if the average company offers its CEO 2.0 times his salary in life insurance versus your 2.2 times. But if your company is giving the CEO a special life insurance policy with a face value of $10 million, well, you'd better account for this difference.

Your input into the survey process is definitely needed. More than any other executive in the company, you are in a position to ensure that your comparator group is representative and that all major forms of compensation are taken into account in measuring the competitiveness of your pay package.

Chapter Three

VALUING COMPENSATION PACKAGES

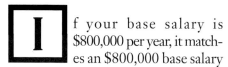f your base salary is $800,000 per year, it matches an $800,000 base salary paid to any of the CEOs included in your survey comparator group. But once you start to measure any other form of compensation, the going gets a lot rougher.

Take the annual bonus, for example. Most people conducting surveys see a $500,000 bonus paid to the CEO of Company A as identical to the $500,000 bonus paid to the CEO of Company B. But that conclusion presupposes that the bonuses contain the same degree of risk. Suppose, however, that in the last three years both Company A and Company B had the following returns on equity: 20 percent, -5 percent, and 10 percent. And suppose that the last three bonuses paid to Company A's CEO were $550,000, $450,000, and $500,000, whereas the last three bonuses paid to Company B's CEO were $800,000, $0, and $500,000. Knowing these facts, do you still believe that the $500,000 bonus paid to the CEO of Company A should be treated the same as the $500,000 bonus paid to the CEO of Company B? The latter, after all, is taking on much more pay risk. And because this is so, his bonus, after adjustment for greater risk, is worth substantially less than that paid to the CEO of Company A.

Getting sufficient information to measure the riskiness of annual bonuses is no easy business. But if you agree to inject more risk into your bonus, you need to make it your business. Otherwise, you will end up paying yourself the same as your counterparts while taking on more risk. You could end up cheating yourself.

Stock options present the thorniest problem of measurement. Of course, you can sidestep the issue by looking only at stock-option gains. There is little to argue about if a CEO clears $1 million on option shares worth $2 million at the time he exercised them. But the information is hardly useful. If the average CEO exercised options with a gain of $1 million, how many new stock-option shares does that suggest your board ought to give you?

I recall a consultant who measured stock-option gains at comparator companies and then asked his client how much appreciation in the client's own stock could be expected during the next five years. If the average option gain among the survey group companies were $1 million, and if the client thought his company's stock might appreciate by $50 per share in the next five years, the consultant recommended an option grant of 20,000 shares. But if the client thought his company's stock might appreciate by only $25 per share, he recommended an option grant of 40,000 shares. God pity the shareholders whose CEO thought the stock might appreciate by only $1 per share during the next five years.

In looking at option gains, you also need to consider that many go unreported. CEOs typically receive option grants right up to their retirement but wait to exercise many of them until several years after retirement. And some option gains that do get reported can be traced back to grants made when the CEO was not the CEO. As a result, option gains tend to be misstated.

That leaves the option grant rather than the option gain. Through surveys your consultant can obtain good information on the size of stock-option grants made to other CEOs while they were CEOs. So the time-lag problem associated with option gains can be eliminated. But an even more vexing question is raised: if the CEO receives an option on 50,000 shares at a strike price (what he has to pay to exercise the option) of $50 per share, and if the stock is selling for $50 per share at the time of the grant, and if the term of the option is 10 years, what is the value of the option at the time of the grant? The gut answer is that the option has no value at all because, were the executive to exercise it, he would receive no gain. But can that answer be true? After all, if options have no value, why do so many executives clamor to receive them?

A book far more comprehensive than this one could be written on how to value an executive stock option. And you as the CEO need not immerse yourself in that arcana. But you should recognize that stock options represent valuable rights, that a value should be placed on them at the time of their grant, and that value ought to be included in any estimate of your compensation package.

Also, different compensation experts can assess a stock option differently. But just because the experts cannot agree doesn't mean that you should ignore the value of a stock option and therefore implicitly count its value as zero when computing the worth of your compensation package. Even the expert with the lowest possible opinion of your stock option would never come close to assigning it a value of zero.

You have two choices. First, you can select a single option-valuation methodology and use it, provided it is somewhere in the mainstream of expert thinking. Or you can submit several hypothetical stock-option transactions to different consulting firms and ask them to place a value on each transaction. Then you can average the resulting values and use that intelligence to assess the stock-option information being collected from your comparator-group companies.

You may interject here that your outside auditor does not require you to charge your company's earnings with the "value" of stock-option grants. So why bother to include any worth for such grants? Because one reason for high executive pay in the U.S. is the reluctance of the accounting fraternity to require companies to charge their earnings for the value of stock-option grants. Their stance ignores the economic realities of an option transaction. In effect, if a CEO exercises an option with a $1 million pretax gain, the shareholders are going to shoulder a pretax cost of $1 million, no matter what the accountants say. If the $1 million doesn't show up as a direct charge against earnings, it will show up as lowered earnings per share, caused by the issuance of more shares. Or if the company funds the transaction by buying back shares from the open market and keeping the net number of shares outstanding the same after the option exercise as before it, the transaction will still show up as lowered cash on the balance sheet, and lowered future earnings.

As it turns out, the issue of stock-option valuation may be resolved by the Securities and Exchange Commission. The SEC intends to develop a standardized option-valuation routine and to mandate its use by companies when informing shareholders how much option grants are worth. Even so, academics and compensation consultants will continue to debate the matter, much as medieval philosophers debated the number of angels that could fit on the point of a pin. But from a practical standpoint, the matter will be resolved.

Grants of restricted stock, or free shares granted on the condition that the CEO remain with the company for a given number of years, are more straightforward from a valuation standpoint. If you are given 50,000 restricted shares, each worth $20 at the time, it is hard to argue that they are not worth $1 million. Of course, you may wish to subject the $1 million to somewhat of a "haircut" since, unlike an ordinary shareholder, you cannot sell the shares for a set period and so have lower liquidity. But the haircut, if reasonably determined, will likely be relatively small— unless the restriction period is unduly long. For example, a few companies lift restrictions only upon the CEO's retirement, rather than after a more normal period of five years. In such cases, the issue of a haircut becomes more than academic.

Fortunately for this chapter and for you, performance-share awards and performance-unit awards are growing less popular. Unless you have lots of time, you won't relish the notion of assigning a value to such awards at the time of their grant. The reason lies in the necessity of assigning probabilities to each possible outcome. Say you get 10,000 performance shares if earnings-per-share growth is 15 percent per year or more for the next three years, 5,000 shares if EPS growth is 10 percent, and no shares if EPS growth is less than 5 percent; you will have to estimate the probabilities of attaining any level of EPS growth between 0 percent and 15 percent. And to add even more fun to the proceedings, you will have to estimate the likely stock prices at the end of the performance measurement period that match your assumptions concerning EPS growth. And finally, you will have to discount back to their present value all the values you estimate, a step that involves determining a discount rate appropriate to the risk being incorporated into the performance-share or performance-unit plan.

A further issue concerns the period over which you are going to amortize the value of a grant. Suppose Company A grants its CEO an option on 50,000 shares each year, whereas Company B grants its CEO an option on 100,000 shares every other year. If the full value is counted in the year of grant, the CEO of Company B may look to be overpaid every even year and underpaid every odd year. In such a case, it would make sense to charge the CEO of Company B with an annualized value based on an assumed grant of 50,000 shares *every* year.

But many companies say one thing and then do another. They say they are going to give their CEO an option grant only every other year, and then they give him a "special, one-time-only" grant in the off year. Moreover, the CEO may retire with unamortized grant values never counted as part of his compensation.

A related issue concerns the so-called mega-grant. For example, Steven J. Ross of Time Warner received an option on 1.8 million shares carrying a strike price of $150 per share. And Anthony O'Reilly of H. J. Heinz received an option on four million shares carrying a strike price of $29.88 per share. Both Time Warner and H. J. Heinz claim that it will be years, if ever, before these two CEOs receive another option grant. From that perspective, it could make sense to amortize the grant over a period of years, not to charge the entire grant value to their compensation in a single year. But over what period of years? Three? Five? The number of years before they reach retirement age?

There is no clear-cut answer. But if you decide to amortize long-term incentive grants, fairness suggests that you use the same rules for each CEO in your comparator group as for yourself. And if you amortize, you are dutybound to charge off unamortized amounts in future years.

Unfortunately, companies like to rationalize here. I know one CEO who received a 50,000-share option grant each and every year. Then one year his board gave him a "one-time, not-to-be-repeated" option grant for one million shares. The grant was on top of his regular 50,000-share grant that year. As it happened, the company surveyed its comparator group every other year, and the year of the special grant coincided with the year the survey was not being conducted. The company thereupon ignored the special grant entirely. Perhaps the sound of a tree falling in the forest doesn't exist if no one is there to hear it. But in this case, the tree fell on the shareholders, and they felt it fall.

Every major compensation element needs to be measured and included in an assessment of pay competitiveness. And every major grant needs to be counted, if not this year, then over a reasonable and defensible period. To do otherwise is to play games with your shareholders' money.

THE MEN WHO MANAGE CESSNA AIRCRAFT COMPANY HAVE HAD ONE THING IN COMMON EVER SINCE THEY WERE BOYS.

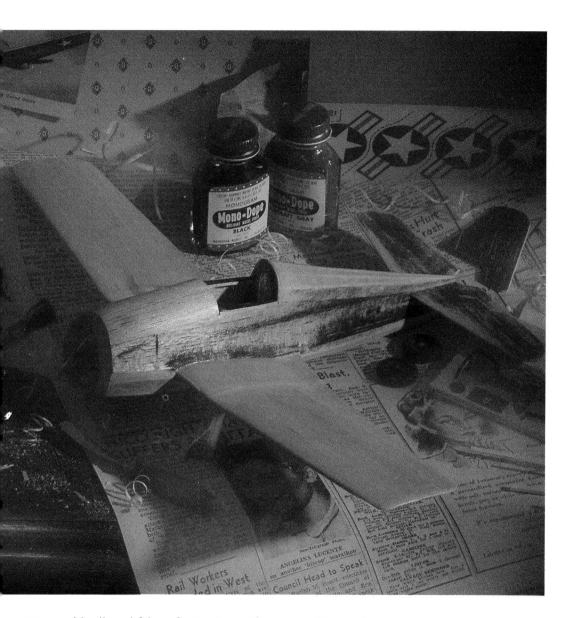

You could call it a lifelong fascination with aviation. You might even call it an obsession. Whatever it is, Cessna's top executives have never outgrown it. All of them are active pilots.

Some would say you don't have to be a pilot to build a good airplane. And they're probably right. But to build a great airplane, we believe it takes something beyond mere aerodynamics and aluminum.

We believe it takes a little passion.

THE SENSIBLE CITATIONS

Cessna
A Textron Company

Chapter Four

DETERMINING YOUR COMPETITIVE POSITION

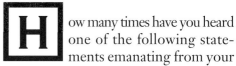ow many times have you heard one of the following statements emanating from your boardroom or from the boardroom of another company: "Our policy is to meet the competitive average," or "Our policy is to pay at the 75th percentile of our comparator group" (higher than all but one quarter of the companies in the group)?

Is it any wonder that CEO pay in America is out of control? For the framers of the above statements forgot to link them to corporate performance. If you say, "Our policy is to meet the competitive average," then you meet that figure whether performance is average, outstanding, or abysmal. The result is that you eliminate any linkage between pay and performance.

The companies that want to pay at the 75th percentile present an added problem. They too fail to specify any linkage between 75th percentile pay and corporate performance. But they also help to ratchet up corporate pay. In a study I conducted a few years back, one-third of 100 companies queried indicated their desire to pay at the 75th percentile of the competitive distribution, while two-thirds indicated their desire to pay at the competitive average. None expressed interest in paying below the average. With that sort of pattern, pay will inescapably rise and rise. And rise and rise it has.

So here is what it takes to compensate yourself both wisely and fairly. First, in linking pay to performance, determine just what you mean by performance. Is performance total shareholder return, counting both stock-price appreciation and dividends? Is it price appreciation alone? Is it return on equity? Or growth in earnings per share? And is it performance during a single year? Or over five years? Or 10 years? Does the definition of performance change according to the type of compensation being examined? For example, is performance defined as growth in EPS when the annual bonus is discussed and as 10-year stock-price appreciation when the stock-option program is discussed?

I cannot give you adequate answers here that will work on a micro level. But on a macro level, the operative phrases are *long term* and *total shareholder return*. If we have learned anything from the Germans and especially the Japanese, it is the notion of patient investing over many years. So paying for short-term as opposed to long-term performance may be worse than not paying for performance at all. Some years ago I worked with Digital Equipment, and I spent a fair amount of time with that company's legendary founder and CEO, Kenneth H. Olsen. Digital did not have an annual bonus plan, and Olsen said that was exactly the way he wanted it. "It's not that I'm afraid annual bonuses won't work," he continued. "It's that I'm afraid they will work—by causing our key people to focus on performance over short periods like one year and by pitting one department against another."

A CEO's pay ought to be highly responsive to long-term performance and less responsive to the short term. By *long term* I am thinking of at least five and perhaps 10 years. If CEOs understand that they will make the most money by increasing the R&D budget rather than cutting it to hype up this year's earnings, they will be well on the way to showing the Japanese and Germans that the U.S. is once again the most formidable of competitors.

If performance over the long term is going to be measured and rewarded, then the choice of the performance measure becomes easy: total shareholder return. Why do investors put money in your company if not to reap stock-price gains and dividends? To be sure, the stock market can be irrational over short periods. How else to explain the 508-point drop in the Dow Jones average on October 19, 1987? But any mathematician will tell you that random variations tend to cancel each other out over time. Although the market may be crazy at any given moment, it cannot be crazy for long.

"It's not that I'm afraid annual bonuses won't work. I'm afraid they will work—by causing key people to focus on performance over short periods."

Kenneth H. Olsen
Chief Executive Officer
Digital Equipment

In my work as a pay analyst, I assess a company's performance by looking only at its total shareholder return. And in measuring shareholder return, I look at the results from 10 different time windows, stretching in one-year intervals from a one-year to a 10-year return. I then develop a weighted-average total shareholder return from all 10 time windows, with more of the weight on the six-through-10-year windows than on the one-through-five-year windows. I don't mean to suggest that my methodology is perfect, but I think it covers most of the bases.

Now, for the sake of argument, let's assume that you buy into my weighted-average total-shareholder-return methodology. Next I would ask you to define a minimum of three levels of corporate performance. For example, you might focus on weighted-average total shareholder return equal to the 25th percentile, the median, and the 75th percentile of your comparator group. Notice that I am not suggesting absolute levels of return, for example, 10, 15, and 20 percent. Predicting absolute levels puts you in the uncomfortable position of predicting the future of the global economy. But you can at least define your performance in *relative* terms—relative, in this case, to the weighted-average total-shareholder-return performance of your comparator group.

Now that you have come this far, you can complete the exercise by linking a desired competitive position to each level of corporate performance. For example, what would be wrong with paying senior executives at the 25th percentile of your comparator group for 25th percentile total-shareholder-return performance, at the 50th percentile for median performance, and at the 75th percentile for 75th percentile performance? Or if you want a higher risk-to-reward profile, you could offer 90th percentile compensation for 75th percentile performance, in return for paying 10th percentile compensation for 25th percentile performance. Either way, you would have linked pay to performance and gone a long way to ensure that you would not, as in the past, be paying the comparator group average for *any* sort of performance.

As I suggested earlier in connection with defining a comparator group, your policy statements concerning pay as a function of corporate performance ought to be written as if for disclosure in your proxy statement. In other words, does your policy meet the shareholder smell test? Indeed, why not consider going all the way and publishing your goals in your proxy statement?

Chapter Five

LOWERING BASE SALARIES

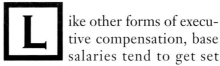ike other forms of executive compensation, base salaries tend to get set through analysis of survey data. So if the average of your comparator group is $800,000 per year, you seriously consider suggesting to your compensation committee that a salary of $800,000 per year would be about right. Or if the average is $1 million per year, you suggest a figure of around $1 million.

How can your logic be faulted? You aren't making up figures of $800,000 or $1 million per year. Those figures represent a statistical distillation of what other companies are actually paying their CEOs for doing the same job.

The logic is not wrong, but the unintended consequences are bothersome. If you earn an annual base salary of $1 million, how can you stand before your shareholders and, with a straight face, tell them your company pays for performance? Even if your company has a bad year, or a series of bad years, and your bonus is cut to zero and your stock options don't pay off, you will still be earning $1 million per year. And a figure as high as $1 million negates your protestations about paying for performance.

The simple solution: cut your base salary. For some years, former senator William Proxmire used to introduce legislation that effectively would have capped CEO pay at the level of *the* CEO, the one who works at 1600 Pennsylvania Avenue. Perhaps Senator Proxmire was being facetious when he introduced this legislation. But what would be wrong with capping a CEO's salary at $250,000, the salary of the president of the United States? Or with establishing a salary as a multiple of the pay of the average-paid worker in your company or of the lowest-paid worker? Ten times the pay of the average-paid worker or perhaps 20 times the pay of the lowest-paid worker might do the trick. Indeed, it might do more than that by keeping you focused on the welfare of your lower-level employees and on the issue of how your pay tracks with theirs. Unfortunately, in years past all of us spent so much time comparing CEO pay at one company to CEO pay at other companies that we overlooked the relationship between CEO and worker pay. In saying this, I don't mean to suggest that some optimum ratio be maintained, because to do so would negate a principle of free markets. But the ratio, whatever it is, ought to be observed from time to time, and if it is growing or shrinking, some thought ought to be given to why this is so.

Now, you may think, *What could be dumber than the ideas just proposed?* If you cut your salary to, say, $200,000 per year, what are you going to do about the salary of your chief operating officer, who currently earns $600,000 per year? And what about the pay of your chief financial officer, who earns $400,000 per year? Indeed, in some companies what about the pay of 100 other executives, all of whom earn more than $200,000 per year?

In the early phase of my consulting career, I did some work for J.C. Penney Inc., then headquartered in New York. I discovered two things early on. First, every employee in the company was called an associate. The purpose was to get Penney employees to avoid the "us against them" attitudes so prevalent between workers and management in other companies. So far as I have gone, the use of "associate" wouldn't seem to represent anything other than a public-relations ploy. But Penney went one step further. No associate in the company earned a base salary of higher than $10,000, not even the associate also titled chief executive officer. As a result, the people at Penney who earned $10,000 were stacked up like cordwood. Nonetheless, the company prospered.

Yet how could that be, when Sears, Roebuck & Company, to name just one competitor, might have been offering salaries that were 20 times higher? The answer is that, although Penney capped executive salaries, it didn't cap executive *pay*. The CEO received a combination of a $10,000 salary and a bonus that made him the highest-paid employee—sorry, *associate*—in the company, and that restored the traditional pay relationships between CEO, chief operating officer, and chief financial officer.

If you think the J.C. Penney analogy is outdated, given that even Penney no longer follows its $10,000-per-year maximum salary policy, take a look at Bear Stearns, the highly successful Wall Street investment-banking firm. There every senior managing director, even the firm's fabled chairman, Alan C. "Ace" Greenberg, earns the same salary of $200,000 per year.

So if you cut your salary from $1 million to $200,000 per year, you don't have to be out $800,000. You can, for example, get the $800,000 back as a higher annual bonus opportunity or in the form of larger-than-normal stock-option grants. Although you may get the lost base salary back, however, you will have changed your risk-reward profile. For in the bad years, your pay will plummet—all the way to $200,000. When your employees and shareholders see the cut you took, how can they, in fairness, say a word when you cart away millions during the good years?

But wait, you will say, taking away $800,000 of base salary and giving back $800,000 of bonus in an average year doesn't compensate me for the fact that my pay package is much riskier than before. And it ignores that if I cut my salary, my pension will drop, and so will my life insurance, and so forth.

If you take on more pay risk, you ought to be entitled to more pay reward. So you're right, it won't do to cut your salary by $800,000 and then raise your average annual bonus by $800,000. Given the greater potential volatility incorporated in your bonus, perhaps it should be raised to $1 million to provide you with an extra reward that offsets the extra pay risk.

As for the lost benefits, these can be restored through supplemental executive benefit plans. Although your actual salary is $200,000 per year, your supplemental pension plan can provide that your salary, for purposes of computing your pension, will be equal to the average paid by the companies in your comparator group—in this case $1 million per year. That way, you will not see your benefits reduced in line with your base salary.

Cutting your base salary, like enjoying Scotch, may be an acquired taste. But if you're truly serious about paying for performance, it's a step to seriously examine.

IN 1995,
PEOPLE AROUND THE WORLD
WILL BEGIN DOING THE SIX-SECOND MILE.

You're looking at the fastest business jet in the world. At Mach .9, it does a mile in 6.06 seconds. And sprints LA-to-New York in under four hours.

It's the new Citation X. And it's the latest example of Cessna's commitment to the development of new technology. Our total investment in business aircraft research and support is now more than a billion dollars.

You can see for yourself the remarkable result of that investment when Citation X deliveries begin in 1995. But you'd better look fast.

THE SENSIBLE CITATIONS

Cessna
A Textron Company

Chapter Six

ADDING ZIP TO THE BONUS PLAN

Most executive bonus plans were designed in the 1940s and '50s, and for a while they worked as expected. The typical plan was funded by a formula approved by the company's shareholders. The company could spend up to $X on executive bonuses, with X determined by first deducting from profits an amount equivalent to a predetermined return on equity and by then appropriating a percentage of the leftover profits for the bonus plan.

To illustrate, a plan might provide that the board could spend 10 percent of after-tax profits on bonuses, after first deducting an amount equivalent to a 6 percent return on average equity. If after-tax profits were $100 million and average equity was $1 billion, an amount equivalent to a 6 percent return on average equity, or $60 million, was subtracted from the $100 million of profits. The residual profit figure of $40 million was multiplied by 10 percent, resulting in a $4 million bonus fund.

Nothing was wrong with the architecture of this formula. It required that executives stand in the hot desert sun until the company earned some minimal return on its shareholders' equity. Then, and only then, did it permit executives to approach the oasis and drink 10 percent of the water.

But something was wrong with the way the formula operated

over time. In the 1950s, a 6 percent after-tax return on equity represented a return about 3 percent higher than the rate for safe government bonds. And a 6 percent after-tax return on equity represented about two-thirds of the median return on equity being earned by companies generally. Changing times have outdated the typical company's bonus-funding formula, but unfortunately the formula has not been altered.

The long-term corporate bond rate is no longer 3 percent; it is about 8 percent. Instead of offering shareholders a return 3 percent above the risk-free rate, the 6 percent minimum has fallen two percentage points below the risk-free rate. Moreover, although the 6 percent rate once represented about two-thirds of the median return on equity, by the period 1985-90 it represented only about 40 percent of a more contemporary median return-on-equity rate of 14.9 percent.

In the meantime, the 10-percent-of-residual-profits figure was also becoming outdated. By 1990, the typical major company may have increased its sales seven to 10 times. Yet the company didn't need seven to 10 times more bonus money in 1990 than it did in 1950. Such a figure would be considerably beyond what could be accounted for by inflation. When a company expands, it adds more employees, but no matter how large it grows, it still has only one CEO, one chief operating officer, and one chief financial officer.

When you lower the minimum return rate in a bonus-funding formula and maintain the percentage of residual profits diverted to executives, you begin to generate surplus funds. And that is exactly what has happened over the years. More often than not, a company's funding formula is a joke. It may produce $100 million in funding, when even the most greedy management would dare take only $30 million in bonuses. Because surplus funding occurs even in a bad performance year, the funding formula fails to enforce the pay-for-performance discipline it was designed to create. And matters worsen when, as happens in more than a few companies, unspent bonus funds can be added to the compensation granary to help out management in years when performance is so bad that even the by-now slushy funding formula fails to generate bonus dollars.

With the formula's discipline lost, the compensation committee became the only bulwark of pay for performance. Of course, when performance was spectacular it was easy for the committee to be reasonably openhanded. But compensation committees are not much different from the rest of us, who, when we receive deplorable service at a restaurant, lose our nerve at the prospect of confronting a hostile waiter with an empty change plate. So mumbling something about the need "to keep our good people," the compensation committee developed the habit of paying the same bonus in good times and bad.

What is needed is to revitalize bonus-funding formulas with the discipline they once exhibited. The typical minimum-profit threshold, instead of being equivalent to a 6 percent after-tax return on equity, ought to equal about a 10 percent after-tax return on equity. A 10 percent return would be about two percentage points higher than the current risk-free rate and about two-thirds of a contemporary median return-on-equity level. In other words, a 10 percent after-tax return on equity in 1992 would contain about the same level of risk as a 6 percent return on equity did in the 1950s.

Companies also need to revisit the percentage of residual profit they are willing to divert to executives. If 10 percent is too high a figure, then lower it to a more realistic level. And surplus funds should not be carried over to fund bonuses when performance is poor. Or if they are carried over to reward a few high-performing people, they should never be spent on the CEO or the other senior executives responsible for the poor year.

This notion of giving a bonus to some but not to the CEO is worth a digression. At Citicorp, neither John Reed nor his top three subordinates earned a bonus for 1990's disastrous performance (earnings per share dropped 51 percent, and the stock tumbled accordingly), nor did they receive any long-term incentive grants. No bonuses were paid to the next 16 ranking executives either, but 14 of them did receive long-term incentive grants. Among executives below the top 20, some received bonuses and long-term incentive grants. Reed's behavior is unusual but also right. Rewarding some employees with a bonus does not automatically justify one for the CEO.

Bringing the bonus formula in sync with economic realities is a useful way to forge a better relationship between company performance and executive bonuses. And as long as you are revising your bonus formula, give some thought to instituting a personal bonus-funding formula for yourself. Such a formula removes you from a conflict-of-interest position when you recommend how much of an overall bonus fund should be diverted to your subordinates versus, implicitly, how much you should receive. Specifically, the personal formula prevents any temptation to hog a greater

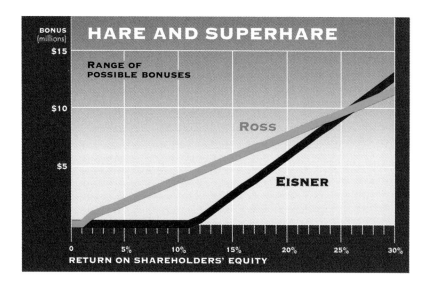

Time Warner and Walt Disney both tie their CEOs' bonuses much more tightly to performance than most companies do, but the volatility is greater at Disney. As the graph shows, at moderate levels of corporate performance, Time Warner's Steven Ross would do better. Michael Eisner gets no bonus until Disney's after-tax profits equal an 11 percent return on shareholders' equity, but after that he gets 2 percent of profits—$4.7 million for fiscal 1991.

◆

percentage of the shrunken fund for yourself in a year of poor performance.

Presumably, your personal-funding formula could feature the same, or an even higher, minimum-profit threshold than the overall funding formula. The particular threshold you select will, in any event, have a pronounced impact on the risk characteristics of the bonus plan. If you follow my earlier advice and pay yourself an ultra-low salary, you'll want to be careful not to inject too much risk in your short-term bonus formula. If you do, you may tilt your incentive toward short-term behavior, with possible adverse consequences for your shareholders. From that perspective, only a modest minimum profit threshold should probably accompany an ultra-low base salary.

To illustrate, let's look at two entertainment industry executives with personal bonus funding formulas—Time Warner co-CEO Steven Ross and Walt Disney's Michael Eisner. Ross is entitled to an annual bonus generally equal to 0.4 percent of pretax profits, provided Time Warner's after-tax profits are equal to at least $75 million. Eisner is entitled to an annual bonus equal to 2 percent of after-tax profits, after first deducting an amount equivalent to an 11 percent after-tax return on average shareholders' equity.

Almost instinctively, you can infer that Eisner's bonus is more leveraged than Ross's, providing him relatively more reward than Ross in years of high performance and less reward in years of low performance. Your instincts are proven correct when you look at the graph on the facing page, which shows the bonuses the two CEOs would receive as a function of varying assumed levels of after-tax return on average equity for 1991. Ross begins to earn a bonus when Time Warner's after-tax return is less than 2 percent, whereas Eisner stands in the hot sun until his company earns an 11 percent after-tax return. (Although Ross's bonus is nowhere near as leveraged as Eisner's, his bonus is much more leveraged than that of the typical CEO, where deviations of more than plus or minus 20 percent from the target bonus are rare.) Notice too that Eisner's 11 percent return-on-equity performance threshold is in line with my earlier recommendation that a contemporary performance threshold would be on the order of a 10 percent return on equity.

A practical demonstration of the leverage in Eisner's bonus can be seen by comparing his bonus for fiscal year 1990 to his bonus for FY 1991. In FY 1990, Disney earned a 25.2 percent return on its average equity, and Eisner received a bonus of $10.5 million. In FY 1991, Disney's return on equity sagged to 17.3 percent (although at 17.3 percent, it still weighed in at the 66th percentile among the 500 most highly capitalized companies). So Disney's return on equity dropped 31 percent between 1990 and 1991. But Eisner's bonus descended even faster—from $10.5 million to $4.7 million, a drop of 55 percent.

"Of course Eisner's bonus dropped," you may snort, "but he's still left with a bonus of $4.7 million, and that's one hell of a lot higher than almost any other CEO in America earns in total compensation, much less in bonus." Perhaps Eisner's bonus is higher than it should be, but his willingness to take risks in his bonus and to some degree in his base salary (which is a relatively low $750,000 and has remained so for seven years) provides a defense for his high pay. Keep in mind that, although Eisner's $4.7 million bonus for FY 1991 was considerably higher than that of almost every other CEO, he still did not take any flak from his shareholders. They seemed satisfied that he took a bonus hit, and they seemed more than ready to wait for this great performer to perform greatly once again. (And perform Disney did, for within six months of the end of FY 1991, the stock rose by more than 50 percent.)

Many CEOs, reacting negatively to the suggestion of a personal bonus formula, will retort that formulas have a way of going awry and are no substitute for the after-the-fact judgment of an informed board. John Reed of Citicorp is one such CEO. Unlike many of his peers, he has been more than willing to take a meat ax to his pay package in response to his company's declining performance. He has gone two years without a pay raise, an annual bonus, or even a new long-term incentive grant. When I asked him why he didn't recommend some pay mechanism that would ensure a rich payout if he was successful in restoring Citicorp to its once preeminent status, he indicated such an action was unnecessary. "I trust my board to recognize my accomplishments," he said. I can only pray that his *Field of Dreams*-like attitude ("If you build it, they will come") pans out. But most boards might not have the guts to give the CEO a large enough reward in a turnaround situation to counterbalance his lean-pay years. After all, the board has no pre-established funding formula to hide behind; it has only its present judgment. For these reasons, a pre-established personal-funding formula, if it incorporates the proper degree of risk and reward, is the best way to ensure that annual bonuses are related to performance.

The adoption of a personal-funding formula carries with it an obligation to keep the formula current, unlike the funding formulas of the 1940s and 1950s. The minimum profit threshold can itself be established by means of a formula, e.g., a return on equity equal to two-thirds of the median return achieved by companies in the comparator group during the last three years. Or the minimum profit threshold could be two percentage points above the average long-term Treasury bond rate during the past two years. As for the percentage of residual profits diverted to the CEO, the compensation committee can adopt certain design principles and stick to them from year to year. For example, the percentage of profits can be whatever provides the CEO with a base salary and bonus package that approximates the 90th percentile of the comparator group distribution. Of course, his company must achieve a return on equity also equal to the 90th percentile returns anticipated by the comparator group during the forthcoming year.

Injecting more swing into an annual bonus might seem at odds with my earlier recommendation that the bulk of incentive emphasis be placed on long-term performance. But I contend that a short-term incentive plan becomes another form of long-term incentive compensation if the CEO knows exactly how his future short-term bonuses are to be calculated. If like Eisner I know that for each of the next 10 years I am entitled to a bonus equal to 2 percent of after-tax net income (after first deducting from net income an amount equivalent to an 11 percent return on average shareholders' equity), then I can, in a highly self-serving way, plot a strategy that will maximize my income over a long period. Viewed from that perspective, I might well decide to take actions that, far from maximizing after-tax profits and therefore my bonus this year, would have the effect of lowering both, in return for a much higher level of after-tax profits and bonuses down the pike.

The purpose of this chapter is not to suggest any precise way to design a personal-funding formula that will work for your company every year. But if you take on a reasonable amount of pay risk—and, like Babe Ruth, point to center field before belting a home run, and thereby define for the crowd just what superlative performance is—you can find a way to get where you want to go. The result will likely be a much higher degree of pay swing than you have heretofore experienced. And that pay swing will reward you more richly than ever when you perform for your shareholders and silence those who have accused you of not playing the pay game fairly.

THE VERY FIRST CITATION PRODUCT
TO GO UP IN THE AIR WASN'T A BUSINESS JET.

Before the first Citation ever rolled off the line, we built the first service center dedicated exclusively to maintaining the aircraft.

Now, nearly 2,000 Citations later, there are Citation Service Centers located 45 minutes apart throughout the contiguous United States, and Authorized Citation Service Stations around the world.

When you own a Citation, we're here to take care of the aircraft so the aircraft and you can do what you do best. Take care of business.

THE SENSIBLE CITATIONS

Cessna
A Textron Company

Chapter Seven

LONG-TERM INCENTIVE PLANS

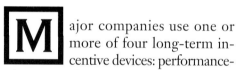ajor companies use one or more of four long-term incentive devices: performance-unit awards, performance-share awards, restricted-stock awards, and stock-option grants.

Performance-unit awards, which offer the executive cash for meeting financial goals, typically over three years, are starting to fall out of favor. Most such plans predicate payouts on earnings-per-share growth; some concentrate on return-on-equity achievements. All suffer from difficulties in deciding on the measure of performance to be "incented" and the degree of stretch to incorporate into the plan targets. So executives may receive large payments for performance that, in retrospect, was not that great. The same executives may finish the next three-year performance cycle and receive nothing, although they did a terrific job. Even more important, performance-unit awards rarely link payouts to the two things shareholders desire most: stock-price appreciation and dividends. So executives may receive large payments at the most inopportune time—when the company's stock price is falling.

Performance-share awards, which offer the opportunity to receive free shares of stock provided certain financial goals are achieved, suffer from one of the two deficiencies of performance-unit awards: they involve difficult financial goal-setting. However, since the medium of payment is free shares of stock and not cash, performance shares at least offer the possibility of more closely aligning the executive's and the shareholders' interests. Nonetheless, few companies grant such awards, in part because of the goal-setting problems and because of the relatively adverse accounting treatment they generate.

Both types of awards are also difficult for affected executives to understand. For example, Lockheed employs a performance-unit plan that measures performance in overlapping three-year periods. One-third of the incentive weight is placed on Lockheed's total-shareholder-return performance in relation to its aerospace competitors and to the Standard & Poor's 400 group of companies. The other two-thirds is placed on internal financial goals, including cash-flow return on assets. Not surprisingly, Lockheed's top management is heavily populated by engineers and other technologists who seem to thrive on such complexity. But Lockheed may revisit its long-term incentive strategy. As its CEO, Dan Tellep, remarked: "Nobody really thinks through the complex formulas of our long-term incentive plan before deciding what actions to take." In other words, if few executives understand how the plan works, how can it motivate them to improve performance?

That leaves the long-term incentive field mainly to the two remaining devices: restricted-stock awards and stock-option grants.

Although stock-option plan designs vary, the vast majority of companies granting stock options set the option's strike price to equal the market price on the grant date. They also give the executive 10 years to exercise the option. As for restricted stock, most companies give the shares to the executive and throw in voting rights and dividends to boot. Restrictions on the free-share awards typically lapse over five years, although a few companies continue restrictions until the executive's retirement. In almost every case, remaining with the company is the sole requirement for earning the shares. So the executive need not perform, only exist for the requisite period.

Restricted stock has taken a lambasting in the business press, and yours truly has been one of the most vociferous critics. Why? Because with a restricted-stock grant, the executive stands to earn money for unacceptable performance. If the company's stock price drops in half following a grant of restricted shares, the executive still receives a payout, since he spends nothing for the shares in the first place. And, of course, he also receives the dividends.

This problem of restricted stock can be illustrated by comparing grants of restricted stock to grants of stock-option shares. Faced with a choice of receiving 1,000 restricted shares or 1,000 option shares, any executive who chooses the latter should be fired for stupidity—and with alacrity. Consider the three components of share ownership: the original share value at the time of the grant, the future appreciation or depreciation in the stock price, and the future dividend stream. With a restricted-stock grant, the executive receives all three components. With a stock-option grant, he receives only the future stock-price appreciation. Consequently, one stock-option share is worth far less than one restricted share. How much less depends on a number of considerations, including the ratio of the strike price to the market price at the time of the grant, the estimated future yield of the stock, the estimated future rate of return on a risk-free investment, the length of the stock-option term, and, in some option valuation models, the estimated future volatility of the company's stock prices.

Delving into the arcana of option valuation is beyond the scope of this short book. However, if we take a typical stock among the 500 most highly capitalized companies and value it using accepted option-valuation techniques, we can determine that the value of the option on one share is equal to roughly 34.1 percent of the value of a restricted-stock share. Or stated differently, a company would have to grant an executive 2.93 times more option shares than restricted shares to make the game worth playing.

Accepting this 2.93-times ratio, let's give a hypothetical executive a grant of 20,000 restricted shares and 58,600 stock-option shares. Then let's assume that all dividends on the restricted shares are reinvested in more company shares. What happens to executive payouts under the two long-term incentive plans and as a function of various assumed rates of shareholder return during the 10-year life of the stock-option grant? The results can be seen in the graph on the facing page. What this exhibit shows is the greater risk associated with a stock option compared to a restricted-stock grant. At low levels of future company performance, the executive earns more from a 20,000-share restricted-stock award than from a 58,600-share stock-option grant. But the reverse occurs at higher levels of performance.

Several of my studies have shown that restricted stock is associated with relatively poor company performance. Not every company that grants restricted stock is imbued with canine characteristics, but enough are to produce the findings just cited. A likely reason for the phenomenon shows up in the graph. If you

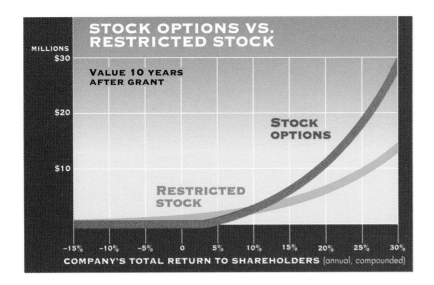

Because the recipient owns the shares but gets them free, restricted stock pays off no matter how the other shareholders fare. Conventional stock options don't pay off until other shareholders profit. As their returns rise, however, options quickly become much more valuable. The graph compares a grant of 20,000 restricted shares that pay a 3.2 percent annual dividend to an option on 58,600 shares (see text).

◆

are running a company and are not terribly bullish on the prospects for your stock, why take a 58,600-share stock-option grant? Instead, take a 20,000-share restricted-stock grant. That way, if your bearish predictions come true, you will be better off. To put it another way, the same element of adverse selection is operating here as with long-term disability insurance. Those who apply for and receive such insurance typically experience a higher rate of future long-term disability than those who do not. And those who opt for restricted-stock grants seem to experience a higher rate of future long-term corporate disability.

Restricted stock has no valid role in the compensation package of CEOs and other senior executives, except as a payment for incentive awards earned under other circumstances. Consider Michael Eisner. As already mentioned, he is entitled to a bonus equal to 2 percent of Disney's after-tax profits, after first deducting an amount equivalent to an 11 percent after-tax return on Disney's average shareholder's equity. Eisner's arrangement also provides that he receive his bonus in cash until Disney's after-tax return reaches 17.5 percent. Any further bonus is paid in shares of restricted stock. So Eisner is effectively compelled to invest part of his bonus in company shares. That investment, in turn, heightens his sensitivity to Disney's future performance.

Johnson & Johnson and a number of Wall Street investment-banking firms are also forcing senior executives to take a large part of their bonuses in restricted-stock grants. Chevron's Keller, among others, feels that this is an appropriate use of restricted stock. "Paying a bonus that has otherwise been earned on the basis of performance in shares of restricted stock," he said, "helps the same dollars do double duty."

If performance-unit and performance-share awards have begun to fall into disuse, and if CEOs ought to avoid restricted-stock grants, the stock option wins as the long-term incentive of choice. However, stock-option grants are not without serious flaws. First, the market price on the grant date may not be representative of the company's past stock prices. If the strike price is unrealistically high or low, what an executive makes from the option grant may be unrelated to the company's performance.

Second, when to exercise the options is left largely to the executive. Typically, exercise restrictions lapse four years after the grant, leaving the executive a corridor of six years to decide when to purchase his shares. And who knows better than the CEO when the time is ripe? Could a CEO, bearish about the future of his company's stock price, decide to exercise right now, benefiting from what may be an all-time high price? I have no research to prove my point, but *The Wall Street Journal* faithfully reports on executives who exercise their stock options, presumably on the assumption that it is providing valuable market intelligence to its readers. Consider also that shorter exercise restrictions help undermine the long-term incentive intent of the plan by allowing the executive to take advantage of what may be randomly generated rather than results-generated market highs.

Third, although a stock option may align the executive's and shareholders' interests when the stock price is rising, it does no such thing when the price is falling. The shareholder loses real money; the executive simply fails to exercise his stock option.

Fourth, when the stock price does fall, some companies, although fortunately not many, invite their executives to turn in their option agreements for revision. The revision consists of lowering the strike price of their shares to the current, and lower,

PERHAPS THE MOST IMPORTANT THING WE BUILD AT THIS CESSNA PLANT IS HUMAN POTENTIAL.

A year ago, this Cessna worker was considered unemployable. Lacking skills and education, she and her children lived on welfare checks.

But a new program, initiated by Cessna Aircraft Company, changed all that. The program provides job training for the undereducated. It gives each person a basic skill, a means to make a living, and a source of pride.

Graduates of the program now build high-quality parts for Cessna and, at the same time, something even more valuable. Better lives for themselves.

THE SENSIBLE CITATIONS

Cessna
A Textron Company

market price. Indeed, some companies have offered their executives so-called option swaps four times within a relatively short period. One company offered two option swaps in the same fiscal year. Warner-Lambert's retired CEO, Joseph D. Williams, spoke for all the executives I interviewed when he said: "We never made a swap when I was CEO. We simply didn't believe in them. If options are under water [where the current market price has dropped below the option's strike price], so be it. We didn't perform, did we?"

Fifth, in the last few years we have witnessed the emergence of the so-called mega-option grant. So, for instance, a food-company CEO receives an option on four million shares carrying a strike price of $29.88 per share. And a shoe-company CEO receives an option on 2.5 million shares carrying a strike price of $17.88 per share.

The problem with mega-grants reminds me of the difficulties many manufacturing companies encounter when they move from pilot to mass production. If the size of the option grant is relatively small, problems associated with it are small. If the CEO receives a grant of 50,000 shares, and the stock price rises only from $30 to $40 in 10 years—an unacceptable compounded annual appreciation rate of 2.9 percent—he makes $500,000 that he shouldn't have made. But that's small potatoes compared with the 10-year aggregate value of his pay package. Not so, however, if the option grant is for four million shares. In that case, the CEO receives $40 million of extra pay for growing the stock price at a piddling rate of 2.9 percent per year.

Given all these contaminants, the relationship between stock-price appreciation and an executive's gain from exercising stock options is exceedingly tenuous. In one study of 187 CEOs, I found that knowing the company's past rate of stock-price appreciation was helpful in explaining only 11 percent of the variation in option gains. In other words, 89 percent of the variation had nothing to do with stock-price appreciation, the one thing that ought to account for all of the variation in option gains.

A further problem with stock options must also be noted. Shareholders want stock-price appreciation and dividends, and except for possible differences in tax treatment, they are indifferent about which they receive. Indeed, most shares in this country are owned by institutions, which pay no taxes on either.

But an executive with a stock option is not indifferent to stock-price appreciation versus dividends. The reason? He receives the former and not the latter. Consider the resulting conflict for the executive. Suppose that a company can optimize its total shareholder return by offering its shareholders a 3 percent yield and by working to increase its stock price at the annual rate of 9 percent. In this scenario, shareholders experience a 12 percent per year total shareholder return. Now suppose that the company decides to eliminate its dividend and retain the earnings previously paid in dividends. However, the company has no good uses for the incremental retained earnings and keeps them in short-term commercial paper or invests them in projects that promise only marginal returns. In either event, the effect on total shareholder return will not be wondrous to behold. Instead of earning a total shareholder return of 12 percent per year, consisting of 9 percent stock-price appreciation and a 3 percent dividend yield, total shareholder return is now, say, 11 percent per year—11 percent stock-price appreciation and no dividend yield. The shareholders end up the losers. But the executives in the company win, because the only component of shareholder return they care about, stock-price appreciation, has risen from 9 to 11 percent.

A further problem related to long-term incentive plans involves charges to earnings. Some plans have prettier accounting treatment than others. If you pay an executive $1 million in cash under a performance-unit plan, you must charge your pretax earnings with $1 million. Or if, under a performance-share plan, you give an executive 20,000 shares then worth $1 million, you must also charge your pretax earnings with $1 million. But if you give an executive a grant of restricted shares worth $500,000, and if the shares double in value to $1 million by the time the restrictions lapse, you need to charge your pretax earnings with only $500,000, not $1 million. And finally, if you give an executive a stock option that yields a pretax gain of $1 million, you need not charge your earnings with a single penny.

These inconsistencies in accounting treatment have caused not a few CEOs to conclude that restricted stock is "cheaper" than performance units and performance shares and that stock options may even be costless, since there is no earnings statement impact at all.

Ask any economist, however, and he will tell you that if you give an executive a pretax benefit of $1 million, the cost to the shareholders will be $1 million. That's true whether the benefit is in performance units or performance shares, which result in a $1 million charge to earnings, or in restricted shares, which result in a $500,000 charge to earnings, or in option shares, which result in no charge at all. As noted earlier, compensation cost is felt in one or more of three ways: through a charge to earnings, through an increase in the number of shares outstanding, or a diminution in cash. The cash loss occurs if the company buys back shares on the open market to keep the number of shares outstanding the same after the issuance as before it.

Still, although the economic impact may be the same, the accounting impact is not. Because this is so, CEOs have developed a fondness for restricted stock and a downright lust for stock options. These forms of compensation indisputably make the company's income statement look less bad. But there is little reason to believe a "less bad" income statement translates into a higher stock price. Statistics on the number of shares under option or granted under restricted-stock plans are routinely reported in footnotes to the annual report. One has to suppose that sophisticated financial analysts consider these numbers when determining their buy-and-sell recommendations. From that standpoint, the stock market looks beyond a company's income statement to its true economic condition. If this viewpoint is correct, and a growing body of empirical evidence suggests that it is, it doesn't matter a damn whether that $1 million of pretax benefits is charged to earnings. Consequently, adopting a compensation plan solely because it allows for good accounting treatment makes little sense.

Having just argued that charges to earnings don't matter, let me reverse myself and argue that costs under executive compensation plans should be charged to earnings uniformly. Such an approach would carry two advantages. First, a level playing field would end the temptation to adopt a plan solely because its accounting treatment is better. Second, and most important, charging everything to earnings creates a measure of needed discipline and exposes the true costs of an executive's pay package. That may not be welcome news to some CEOs, but it definitely treats the shareholders more fairly.

A final problem is associated with current long-term incentives and the proliferation of such plans. Before the early 1970s, almost all companies operated with a single long-term incentive plan— the stock option. But as the stock market slumped, many companies adopted performance-unit plans to reward executives for nonmarket types of performance such as earnings-per-share growth and return on equity. The problem was that those companies rarely cut back on the size of their stock-option grants. So now they had two long-term incentive plans instead of one. And they now had much higher total compensation for their senior executives, including their CEO. Other companies adopted restricted-stock plans, also without cutting back on the size of their stock-option grants. The result, once again, was long-term incentive-plan proliferation and higher executive compensation. Indeed, a few indefatigable pioneers even adopted three forms of long-term incentive compensation—for example, stock-option grants, restricted-stock awards, and performance-unit awards.

Because hardly any company cut back on existing plans when adopting a new long-term incentive plan, I discovered a handy way to predict whether a CEO would turn up high or low in a compensation survey. Count the number of long-term incentive plans and add 32 percent to the CEO's total compensation package for each long-term incentive plan. The result, statistically, is that a chief executive who participates in no long-term incentive plans is paid 32 percent below the market, a CEO in a single long-term incentive plan is paid at the market, a CEO in two long-term incentive plans is paid 32 percent above the market, and a CEO in three long-term incentive plans is paid 64 percent above the market. Unhappily, all those extra long-term incentive plans, far from spurring the CEO on to greater performance, seem to have increased costs and lowered shareholder returns. Other things being equal, the record shows that you can subtract 1.4 percentage points from a company's 10-year, compounded annual-shareholder-return rate for each long-term incentive plan in which the CEO participates.

The lesson is that if you and other senior executives decide to participate in more than a single long-term plan, you need to make sure you are not simply increasing the size of the compensation package to unreasonable levels.

Better yet, why not cut back to a single long-term incentive plan? There is no valid reason that more than one plan is necessary. Multiple plans may enrich compensation consultants, accountants, and lawyers—and CEOs too—but, on the evidence, what the consultants, accountants, lawyers, and CEOs gain, the shareholders lose.

THE DAY A BUSINESS JET TAUGHT
THE SHISHMAREF FIRST-GRADE CLASS.

The Citation V's unique ability to fly long distances yet land on short airstrips has allowed it to get into some pretty remote places. One such place was the tiny, isolated town of Shishmaref, near the Arctic Circle.

When the Citation landed on a narrow snowplowed strip, children came running from the nearby school. They'd never seen a jet before.

And chances are, they may never see any others besides Citations. Unless Shishmaref builds a runway long enough for less versatile business jets to use.

THE SENSIBLE CITATIONS

Cessna
A Textron Company

Chapter Eight

THE PERFECT LONG-TERM INCENTIVE PLAN

I n Chapter Seven I fired torpedoes at the four major forms of long-term incentive compensation: performance shares, performance units, restricted stock, and stock options. People complain that it's easy to be a critic, and now that I am one, I admit the complaint has merit. For the hard part, after criticizing current practice, is to suggest a better way to pay executives—to design the perfect long-term incentive plan.

Setting forth a cast-in-concrete design that would apply to every company in every circumstance is tempting. But to do so would be rank arrogance. No long-term incentive plan is perfect for all companies in every season. But some principles can inform the design of new long-term incentive plans and help such plans do what they are supposed to do—namely, motivate behavior that leads to long-term increases in shareholder value.

Three catch phrases tell the story: *total shareholder return, long term*, and *minimal performance*.

As the CEO of a corporation, you have been hired by a board elected by shareholders interested in building their wealth. Now, an increase in earnings per share and a solid return on equity may be two ways of doing that. But they are means to an end, not an end in themselves. The end is the creation of shareholder value, i.e., increasing your company's stock price and paying dividends, the two components of total shareholder return.

Your perfect long-term incentive plan ought to be geared to increasing total shareholder return. So we can eliminate all four current forms of long-term incentive compensation. Stock options offer an incentive for only one component of total shareholder return—stock-price appreciation. Restricted-stock awards produce payouts for the executive even if total shareholder return is negative. Performance-share awards, like stock options, also incent stock-price appreciation but not dividends. And performance units incent neither stock-price appreciation nor dividends.

The second catch phrase, *long term*, means what it says. Any long-term incentive plan worthy of its name must encourage CEOs to make risky but still prudent decisions aimed at maximizing long-term profitability, even if the result is to depress profits temporarily. So a long-term incentive plan that pays for performance over a relatively short period is no long-term incentive plan; it is a short-term incentive plan.

The number of years of performance an incentive plan should capture before it can be considered long term is arguable. Part of the argument is industry related. Take a retailer like Wal-Mart and a pharmaceutical company like Pfizer. If we identify the key strategic decisions in each company and measure the time between the decision and its measurable results, we find a vast time disparity. Opening a new store is a long-term decision for Wal-Mart. From the moment staff studies are initiated until local officials cut the ribbons can't be much more than three years. But in the pharmaceutical business three years is an eye-blink. During much of the 1980s, Pfizer plowed huge sums of money into its R&D efforts. As a consequence, net income was a lot lower than it might have been. But as the 1990s rolled in, the doors of Pfizer's laboratories opened wide, and a cornucopia of hot new drugs rolled out. Pfizer's stock price took off like an F-16; it almost tripled in the four years after the 1987 market crash.

For a Wal-Mart, a long-term incentive plan that paid for performance over three to five years would likely match the time frames of key strategic decisions. But for a Pfizer—or to use another long-term business, a Boeing—a plan that paid for performance over seven to 10 years would be needed. A lesson here is not to ape the practices of the median company or adopt a one-size-fits-all plan but to tailor the plan to your company.

The third catch phrase is *minimal performance*. It is not acceptable to offer a CEO extra pay for producing just any positive shareholder return. If a shareholder has $100, he can call his local Federal Reserve Bank and place it in risk-free government securities with no commission charge, and the shareholder can sleep soundly knowing his $100 is earning some return. So why should a shareholder be interested in giving a CEO extra reward for moving the stock price from $100 to $105 over five years, when during the same period his $100 investment could increase to, say, $135 without the sinking feeling that so often accompanies stock-price volatility?

Now let's put the three catch phrases—*total shareholder return*, *long term*, and *minimal performance*—together into a prototypical long-term incentive plan design. We will pretend here that we are working with a company that, like a Pfizer or a Boeing, has long strategic decision time frames. A new CEO has just been elected and the stock price is $50 per share. If I were the chairman of the compensation committee of this company's board, this is what I would like to tell the new CEO:

> Today we are giving you a huge stock-option grant on 500,000 shares of company stock. You will not be given any other long-term incentive awards, including stock options, for five years. Moreover, you will not be permitted to exercise any shares until eight years after the grant. Thereafter, you will have two years to exercise your option before it expires.
>
> Today's price is $50, but the strike price will be $92.55. This price—85 percent higher than our present stock price—incorporates an 8 percent minimum compounded annual rate of total shareholder return between now and eight years from now, when you can begin to exercise your option. This 8 percent rate was chosen because our shareholders could, if they wished, invest their money in long-term, zero-coupon government bonds and receive a compounded return rate of about the same 8 percent.
>
> If the stock price was abnormally high when you took over, however, the board might be willing to adjust the strike price. But the evidence that the stock price was not representative would have to surpass seven on the Richter scale.
>
> Because we want this new stock option to incorporate an incentive for total shareholder return, counting both stock-price appreciation and dividends, and not an incentive merely for stock-price appreciation, we will lower your strike price by the amount of dividends declared during the term of your stock-option grant. If next quarter the company declares a dividend of 50 cents per

share, your strike price of $92.55 will be reduced to $92.05. If the quarter after that the company declares a dividend of 60 cents per share, your strike price will be reduced to $91.45.

Five years from today, the compensation committee will review your performance, examine competitive pay levels, and consider granting you another large option. If granted, we will establish its strike price through a two-step process. First, we will take the $50-per-share market price of the stock that prevailed on the date you became CEO and increase it at the rate of 8 percent per year for five years. That action will incorporate the minimum return rate of 8 percent per year that prevailed when you received your first stock-option grant, producing an adjusted strike price of $73.47 per share. Then, assuming that investors can continue to receive an 8 percent return on long-term government bonds, we will increase the $73.47 by a further 8 percent per year for eight years to produce the strike price of your second option grant—$135.99. This price will prevail even if your performance has been so excellent during the past five years that the current price exceeds $135.99 per share. But it will also prevail if the current price is below the $50 it was selling for five years earlier. Once again, your second option grant will not be exercisable for eight years, and then it will be exercisable for two years. Should you retire before any option grant becomes exercisable, the conditions of the grant continue unchanged.

What have we accomplished? First, by crediting the CEO with dividends declared during the term of the option grant, we have established the incentive as total shareholder return and not merely stock-price appreciation. Second, by providing that the CEO cannot exercise the option until eight years after its grant, we have created a true long-term incentive. Third, by establishing a materially higher strike price than the market price at the date of the grant, we have ensured that the CEO will not earn any compensation unless the company's future total shareholder return exceeds what an investor could have earned by placing his fund in safe long-term government bonds. Fourth, by giving the CEO a huge grant upon his election, we have sharpened his interest in moving the company forward. And fifth, by establishing the strike price of any future option grants in a way that incorporates a minimal future return rate and a minimum return from the first day of the CEO's tenure, we make it impossible for him to profit by a drop in stock price after he becomes CEO and also offer him an added reward if he produces total shareholder returns in excess of the minimum return rate. In short, we have related pay to performance, and most important, long-term pay to long-term performance.

You can get a sense of the incentive leverage in the above transaction by referring to the graph on the facing page. There I have started with a 60,000-share, conventional stock-option grant. By *conventional* I mean that the strike price has been set to equal the assumed market price of $50 per share at the time of the grant. I have then structured a 213,821-share grant based on a strike price ($92.50 per share) 85 percent higher than the $50 market price. Many more shares are required under this nonconventional alternative to provide the CEO with the same present value as the conventional grant. Finally, both grants have been assumed to carry a 10-year term of exercise, and exercise has been assumed not to occur until the end of the 10 years.

Combining a strike price 85 percent higher than the market price with many more shares offers the CEO a great deal more reward opportunity under good performance conditions. It also imposes a penalty if performance is poor. Yet even a brief look at this graph shows much more upside reward in the nonconventional option than downside risk. Indeed, the equilibrium point—the point at which the transactions produce the same gain for the executive—occurs at a compounded annual price-appreciation rate of only 8.1 percent.

If you recoil at the notion of setting a strike price 85 percent higher than the current market price, you can ease yourself into the idea by following the lead of AT&T. Although the scheme AT&T has adopted is not altogether new, the fact that such a conservative giant adopted it is of major importance.

AT&T has granted what I will call *tranche options*. Robert Allen, AT&T's CEO, just received a mega-grant of 250,000 option shares. The grant is not expected to be repeated, although Allen and other senior executives will continue to receive regular and more conventionally sized option grants in future years. At the time the grant was made, AT&T's stock price was $38.63 per share, and 25 percent of the 250,000 shares Allen received carried a strike price of the same $38.63 each. Not much new there. But hold on. Another 25 percent of the shares carried a strike price 20 percent higher than AT&T's current market price—$46.35 per share. A third tranche, also consisting of 25 percent of the 250,000 shares, carried a strike price 30 percent higher than the $38.63 base price—

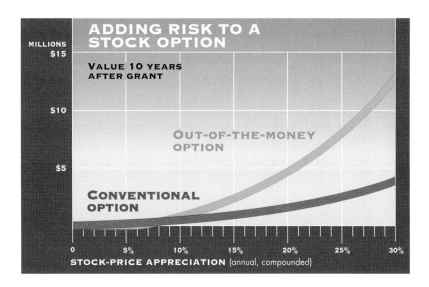

The conventional option can be exercised at its grant-date price. The "out-of-the-money" option can be exercised at a price 85 percent higher, so it's not worth exercising after 10 years unless the stock has risen more than 6 percent a year, compounded. If the stock has risen more than that, though, the out-of-the-money option is where the big reward is. The key: in order to keep the present value of the two grants even, the out-of-the-money grant is for a lot more shares.

◆

$50.21 per share. Finally, the fourth tranche, 25 percent of the 250,000 shares, carried a strike price 50 percent higher than the $38.63 base price—$57.94 per share.

How would the effect of AT&T's tranche-option grant compare to that of a conventional option grant (where the shares carry a strike price equal to the market price on the date of grant) and a restricted-stock grant? Let's assume that the size of both grants has been adjusted to match the present value of AT&T's tranche-option grant; that requires a lot fewer conventional option shares and a still smaller number of restricted shares. As expected, the tranche options link their payouts much more closely to corporate performance than the others do: the addition of each tranche greatly increases the reward for good performance and the risk for bad. At the other extreme, the restricted stock rewards the chief executive even for lousy returns to shareholders.

When it came to approving AT&T's mega-grant of tranche options, an influential member of the compensation committee was Joseph Williams. In 1985, shortly after Williams became Warner-Lambert's CEO, his board approved a mega-option grant. Williams credits the grant with helping unite a top management group that went on to produce spectacular shareholder returns. He feels that AT&T's tranche-option grants can produce similar results. In AT&T's case, he noted: "The timing of the mega-grant was dictated by the acquisition of a huge company [NCR], as well as the acquisition from the outside of several key senior executives, including a chief financial officer. With this one-time grant, we have, effectively, lined up the whole new AT&T top management team, fired the gun, and set them all running together."

General Dynamics' directors also adopted this sort of thinking. They decided to make mega-grants of stock options and to institute a new form of long-term incentive compensation right after they elected a new CEO, William A. Anders. General Dynamics was facing turmoil as a result of cutbacks in the defense budget, and Anders had been hired to lead the company through a mine field of potential problems. Anders and his team did so well his first year that the stock price more than doubled. That stock-price growth was bested by only 2 percent of other major companies. Given the volatility of the defense business, it may turn out that the one-year stock-price performance was a flash in the pan. But at this writing, that has not materialized, and the notion of lining up a new management team and giving it a huge dose of incentive compensation seems to be garnering increasing empirical support.

A final point concerns setting the size of long-term incentive opportunities. A certain perversity operates here, a perversity discovered by Stephen O'Byrne, a consultant with Stern Stewart. To illustrate, let's assume that Company A's book value per share (shareholders' equity divided by shares outstanding) is $12.50. Analysts expect the company to increase its EPS annually by 20 percent and earn a 25 percent after-tax return on equity. Because their predictions are so glowing, the stock trades for four times its book value per share, or $50. At that price, buyers of the stock are expected to earn a 15 percent compounded annual return.

However, the analysts are not thrilled by the prospects of Company B, whose book value per share is $50—four times Company A's book value per share. They figure the company's EPS will increase only 3 percent annually, and consequently its return on equity will begin to slide. If Company B's stock were to trade at the same multiple of book value as Company A's, buyers could expect to earn little on their investment. But the gloomy forecast has depressed Company B's market-to-book ratio to one—a stock price of $50 per share—thereby offering stock buyers the opportunity to earn the same annual return of 15 percent forecast for Company A's investors.

While the analysts were making their predictions, the companies were offering their CEOs option grants of 30,000 shares at $50 each. Here we come to the point. Let's say both companies perform as predicted, and the shareholders of each earn their expected 15 percent annual return. Both CEOs earn the same compensation from their stock-option grants. Yet isn't that perverse? Should the CEO of Company A, who has performed outstandingly, receive the same compensation as the CEO of Company B, who has performed deplorably?

One solution to this problem is to inspect the ratio of a company's stock price to its book value per share. The median company among the 500 with the highest market capitalization is trading at a market-to-book ratio of 1.7 to 1. As just mentioned, companies with higher-than-median ratios generally get those ratios because analysts see their future performance as more like that of Company A. Companies with lower-than-median market-to-book ratios generally get those ratios because analysts see their future performance as more like that of Company B. So a company with a higher-than-median market-to-book ratio should increase the CEO's long-term incentive opportunities so that he can achieve an above-average competitive position. A company with a lower-than-average market-to-book ratio ought to decrease the CEO's long-term incentive opportunities to give him a below-average competitive positioning. Then, if Company A achieves its bullish forecast, and if Company B achieves its bearish forecasts, the CEO of Company A will receive, as he should, substantially more compensation than the CEO of Company B.

Embedding some or all of these "perfect incentive plan" principles in your company's long-term incentive plan will hurt your pocketbook when performance is poor. But if you are a good performer, you can relax. Over the long run, and it is the long run we want to incent, you are going to become seriously rich.

EARLY IN HIS CAREER, MR. PALMER TURNED IN HIS CONVENTIONAL DRIVER FOR SOMETHING WITH CONSIDERABLY MORE LOFT.

Years ago, Arnold Palmer quit using automobiles for traveling to golf tournaments. For almost as long as we have built Citation business jets, Arnold Palmer has flown them.

Without the speed, convenience and reliability of Citations, Arnie says he couldn't possibly compete on the tour, design more than 100 golf courses, and manage his far-ranging business activities.

Mr. Palmer's game is golf, but his business is winning. So is his business jet.

THE SENSIBLE CITATIONS

Cessna
A Textron Company

Chapter Nine

HOLDING THE COMPANY'S STOCK

What's a CEO to do? On the one hand, finance professors and the Wall Street crowd preach the virtues of portfolio diversification. If anyone needs to think about diversification, it's your typical CEO. Most of his net worth may be tied up in restricted-stock grants or in unexercised in-the-money options (options on stock that has a current market price exceeding the strike price). On the other hand, motivational experts, especially professors Michael Jensen and Kevin Murphy of the Harvard Business School, are retailing the notion that if anything executives own too few company shares.

Many executives in many companies do go out of their way to avoid holding company shares. Until the Securities and Exchange Commission changed its insider-trading rules, most major companies attached stock-appreciation rights to stock-option grants. The SARs permitted the executive to receive option profits in cash without borrowing money by exercising option shares, holding them for six months to avoid insider-trading regulations, and finally selling them. With the new SEC regulations, however, the executive may now sell the shares right after their exercise. Either way, executive-share ownership does not increase.

At the opposite end of the share-retention spectrum is John Reed. Not only has he hung on to every share he's earned through company compensation plans, he has done the unthinkable and used $2.5 million of his own funds (mostly borrowed, and not from his own bank) to buy even more Citicorp shares.

Adopting a middle-ground stance on this issue, some companies encourage executives to retain shares acquired through company compensation plans but do not push them to buy more. Sometimes the encouragement borders on compulsion. At one major pharmaceutical company, oral tradition holds that when you exercise a stock option, you may sell sufficient shares to pay back the bank for the loan you took out to handle the exercise. You may also sell sufficient shares to pay the taxes due on the exercise. But if you want a decent career, you'd better not sell any more. To illustrate, assume that an executive exercises a 10,000-share option. His strike price is $50, and the market price at exercise is $120. The executive borrows $500,000 to fund the exercise, and in return he receives certificates for 10,000 shares. He then instructs his broker to sell 4,167 shares. The proceeds are $500,000 (ignoring transaction costs), and the executive uses these to pay off his loan. While instructing his broker to sell 4,167 shares, the executive also tells him to sell a further 2,042 shares. The proceeds are $245,000, sufficient to pay the taxes on the $700,000 option gain. (I am here assuming a 35 percent combined federal and state income tax rate.) Having sold 4,167 shares to pay back the bank and a further 2,042 shares to pay taxes, the executive is left with 3,791 shares worth $454,920, his after-tax gain from the stock-option transaction. These shares had better not be sold—or else.

Holding the company's shares can significantly boost the overall effect of stock-incentive programs. Take the 250,000-share tranche option granted to AT&T's Robert Allen. Chapter Eight indicated the sensitivity of that grant to changes in AT&T's total return to shareholders. Now let's assume that Allen also owns outright 100,000 shares of AT&T stock. As you might expect, if AT&T's performance is good, Allen stands to earn even more than before. But when results are poor, he stands to lose real money for the first time. Indeed, if AT&T's performance is poor enough, the losses on Allen's owned shares could dwarf his base salary and bonus. That actually happened to Citicorp's Reed, whose total compensation, including changes in the value of his shareholdings, moved from a positive $4.9 million in 1989 to a negative $6.9 million in 1990.

A middle-ground approach makes the most sense. CEOs definitely ought to own more than a token 100 shares of company stock. But to insist that after paying off bank loans and taxes they sink every last cent in company stock is foolish. Indeed, such an approach could subvert the intended motivation and turn the CEO into a risk-averse decision-maker or, just as bad, a conglomerator. If you are forced to have almost all your assets in company stock options, the only way to reduce the risk in your portfolio may be to make decisions that reduce the overall risk level in the business or to buy companies in other industries and achieve, through the back door, a degree of portfolio diversification.

What does not make sense is to increase a CEO's shareholdings by giving him outsize grants of restricted stock or stock options and then force him to hold the shares. The CEO becomes a major shareholder, but the shareholders get stuck with the bill.

The CEOs I interviewed are, with a single exception, enthusiastic about having senior executives hold a lot of company shares. Disney's Eisner told me: "You've got to put management in as close an alliance with shareholders as you can. Otherwise you'll end up acting like a manager and not like a shareholder." Warner-Lambert's Williams asserted: "The more shares you own outright, the more believable you are in getting people to follow your leadership." John Reed, who borrowed large amounts to buy more Citicorp shares, echoed Eisner: "It was an emotional decision for me. I wanted to create an environment where I could think of myself as working for myself."

Only Edmund T. Pratt Jr., the just-retired chairman of Pfizer, seemed skeptical: "I wouldn't have worked any harder if you gave me a million shares of Pfizer stock. I don't think I would have managed any differently whether or not I had held lots of shares or sold them off."

Perhaps Pratt is right. It is hard to conceive of Eisner or Reed, both fans of heavy executive shareholdings, working any less had they owned only 100 shares. But owning a lot of shares ties you emotionally to the shareholders and may cause a subtle difference in how you manage the company and, particularly, how you relate to your fellow shareholders. Moreover, holding a lot of shares dramatically increases the risk in the CEO's overall compensation package and helps quell the criticism that CEOs get paid too much.

"The more shares you own outright, the more believable you are in getting people to follow your leadership."

Joseph D. Williams
Chairman, Executive Committee
Warner-Lambert

Chapter Ten

DIVISIONAL LONG-TERM INCENTIVES

Y ears ago, when I was a consultant, I had a meeting with Donald Burnham, then the chairman of Westinghouse Electric Corporation. Burnham, flanked by his two vice-chairmen, told me how Westinghouse was organized into four huge groups and something like 19 subgroups and 83 individual profit centers. Lamenting the short- and long-term incentive plans the company had at the time, he told me:

> Take one of our 83 division managers. Let's say he's cooking the books in his division, cutting back on the R&D, shaving the product quality, and so on. The profits in that division boom, and our division manager earns a big bonus, because we reward for divisional performance in our annual bonus plan. The division manager doesn't have much of an incentive to look to the long term, because his long-term incentive consists of an option on Westinghouse stock. Even though he bends his shoulder to the wheel, in a long-term sense, maybe the 82 other division managers don't. Or even if all 83 managers look to the long-term, maybe our stock price will fall out of bed due to a rise in interest rates. In any event, our division manager is a short-term thinker. He milks his business and the profits boom, and pretty soon we promote him to the next level of management. If he has timed it right, his former

division will fall apart the next year, due, of course, to his having milked it for years. But far from damaging his reputation, the collapse will enhance it. His associates will say, "When Joe ran Division A, the profits were terrific. Then Joe left, and what do you know, the division fell apart. That Joe is a miracle worker." Meanwhile, Joe is working his miracles on the next level of management, cutting the R&D and shaving the product quality. And his profits once again boom. And once again we promote him to the next level of management.

To which one of Burnham's vice-chairmen said: "Yeah, Don, he could even work his way up to chairman of the board!"

But Burnham has a point. Give an executive a short-term incentive to do things over which he has a fair degree of control and a long-term incentive to do things over which he has no control, and you get plenty of short-term behavior.

A divisional long-term incentive plan allows a company to get around the problem posed by Burnham. Under such a plan, the head of a company profit center—division or group—can be rewarded for the long-term performance of his center.

The most intelligent long-term incentive designs share a single characteristic: they attempt to determine what the market value of a division would be if it were a publicly traded entity. Determining a division's market value can be accomplished by calling Goldman, Sachs and asking an investment banker for an opinion or by performing elaborate mathematical modeling aimed at determining the factors—such as cash flow, growth in earnings, and return on invested capital—that drive the stock prices of publicly traded companies operating in the same industry as the division.

Once a market value is determined, an incentive plan can be designed that mimics a stock-option plan. An artificial number of "phantom" shares can be established to provide a starting market value per share for the division's phantom stock. The division head can then be given a synthetic stock-option grant carrying a strike price equal to, or preferably higher than, the starting market value per share. And the executive can be given a period during which to exercise his option. Upon exercise, he can be paid his gain in cash or in parent-company shares of equivalent value.

Not every multidivisional company, however, is a viable candidate for divisional long-term incentives. For example, divisions that seem independent of each other may not be. Division A may be buying products from Division B at transfer prices that are not set in a free market. Or Division A and Division B may be required to cooperate in designing and marketing a complementary line of products. For example, Division A may be manufacturing refrigerators and Division B, ranges. It would be nice if the company's refrigerators and ranges looked appealing when side by side. Or Division A and Division B and, indeed, five other divisions may all draw their technology from a corporatewide R&D center. Or the company, like General Electric, may be intent on developing senior managers by constantly moving them from one division to another. If the divisions of a company share people, products, or technology, adopting separate long-term incentive plans for each division may go a long way toward destroying rather than improving the company.

Reinforcing this warning are remarks by Disney's Eisner: "I once got into a conversation with Warren Buffett about this issue, and he told me that Berkshire Hathaway fundamentally pays division managers on their own results. I can see that that approach might well work beautifully for Buffett, because he is running a conglomerate. There just can't be all that much in the way of interdependence between a See's Candy and a Nebraska Furniture Mart [two of Berkshire Hathaway's many operations]. But at Disney, what we do in one division impacts what we do in another. After all, many of the characters in our theme parks came out of our efforts in film and television. And our retail stores, of course, depend for their uniqueness on the creativity exhibited by virtually all our other divisions. So the last thing I would want to do is incent our various profit centers to go their own way."

Lockheed's Tellep has a viewpoint similar to Eisner's, although he speaks more like the engineer he is: "What worries me about putting in divisional long-term incentive plans at Lockheed is that we might end up optimizing the results of each division but, paradoxically, sub-optimizing the results of Lockheed as a whole."

On the other hand, if the divisions are truly independent, divisional long-term incentives may have magnificent motivational results. The powerful medicine of divisional long-term incentives can be illustrated by an experience I had with a major money-center bank a few years back. Among the bank's many subsidiaries was a relatively tiny unit in the business of managing money for pension funds and other fiduciaries. For each of the past 10 years, the subsidiary had been earning after-tax profits of about $300,000. Indeed, if the time line of the company's profits had been an EKG tracing, the patient would have been dead. The key executives

IMAGINE A CITATION THAT'S BEEN FLYING NONSTOP SINCE THE YEAR 1307.

That's how much flight time Citation business jets have logged. The fleet has accumulated an incredible six million hours of service.

It's the equivalent of one Citation flying night and day for 685 years.

It took more than just one to chalk up six million hours, of course. Nearly 2,000 Citations are now in service – the world's largest fleet.

So if you're looking for the business jet that more businesses fly, just look up. Chances are, there's a Citation passing overhead right now.

THE SENSIBLE CITATIONS

Cessna
A Textron Company

of the subsidiary received decent salaries and an annual bonus opportunity. The bonus seemed more affected by the profits of the parent bank, however, than by those of the subsidiary.

The subsidiary executives also received options on the stock of the parent bank. No matter how magnificent their performance as subsidiary executives, they could never move the stock price of an institution that was more than 100 times as big as they were. And no matter how poor their performance, the stock of the parent bank would never drop enough to punish them. In short, they had little in the way of short-term motivation and nothing in the way of long-term motivation.

To change the picture and to help the subsidiary attract a better grade of talent from Wall Street, a plan was designed that gave the subsidiary executives a significant stake in the long-term profitability of the subsidiary, provided the bank first obtained a competitive after-tax return (in this case, 14 percent) on its capital. Thus the bank became a sort of preferred shareholder with a guaranteed rate of return, as well as the majority common shareholder. And the subsidiary's executives became significant minority shareholders.

Immediately after the new plan was inaugurated, behavior in the subsidiary changed markedly. For openers, the plan helped attract some new talent from Wall Street. Second, the subsidiary returned a good portion of its capital to the parent bank. When asked why the capital had not been returned earlier, the subsidiary head replied: "Earlier, I didn't have to pay 14 percent interest on the money." And third, considerable attention was paid to the subsidiary's costs, attention not paid when no monetary incentives were offered to the subsidiary's executives. For example, the subsidiary tried to move out of its plush offices in the bank's headquarters and into a warehouse in a less than desirable part of town. The subsidiary head reasoned that he and his people met with their clients at the clients' locations and so it no longer made sense to spend a fortune on offices. Or at least it no longer made sense when the subsidiary executives could see that as new minority shareholders they were paying a significant fraction of the office costs out of their own pockets.

These and other moves caused a dramatic change in the subsidiary's fortunes. From a year-after-year pattern of earning $300,000 in after-tax profits, the subsidiary earned $1.5 million in after-tax income in the plan's first year. In short, this plan worked; it changed behavior.

Unfortunately, it also changed the behavior of the parent bank's top management. For the sum of the subsidiary head's salary, his bonus, and the increase in the value of his subsidiary shareholdings exceeded the pay of the parent bank's CEO. He was not amused, and a witch hunt ensued. Indeed, the screaming reached such a pitch that the parent bank sold the subsidiary. Its newly resurgent profit record helped the parent bank obtain a high price.

So for divisional long-term incentives to work, the division must not only be an independent entity, the CEO of the parent company must be an independent thinker. He must be willing, as Citicorp's John Reed has been, to see key subordinates earn more than he—at least in years when the division's performance has been outstanding and the parent company's has been poor.

A reporter once asked Babe Ruth how he could justify his $80,000 salary when President Herbert Hoover earned only $75,000. The Babe's reply: "I had a better year than he did." That reason must be accepted instinctively by CEOs if divisional long-term incentives are to work.

At the same time, a company that adopts these incentives must be willing to suit the needs of each division. Some years ago, I talked about divisional long-term incentives with John F. Welch Jr., the chairman of General Electric. Welch thought they might have some promise at GE, then perhaps the world's most diversified company. But he wondered whether GE would end up with "bad managers running bad divisions." How, he mused, would he be able to get a manager running a successful division to go into a poorly performing division and turn it around if he has no hope for a bonus and little in the way of long-term incentive payouts?

Welch raised a good question, but there is also a good answer: act in the same manner as would a sick, publicly owned company trying to lure an outside CEO to turn it around. In such a case, the company might not be able to offer a great deal in salary and bonuses because of constraints on fixed costs and cash. But it could, and probably would, offer the new CEO a ton of stock-option shares. In effect, the CEO would be asked to assume an abnormally high degree of compensation risk in return for a level of compensation payout that, if the turnaround occurred, would also be abnormally high. That scenario materialized when Iacocca joined Chrysler for $1 per year and a monster stock-option grant.

These same principles could be designed into divisional long-term incentive plans. Although one division of the company might have a more normal risk-to-reward profile, the turnaround candidate would lure its savior by offering him a lot of risk but also the chance to become rich.

As it turned out, Welch decided not to institute long-term incentives at GE. He solved the problem by divesting the company of many of its divisions and concentrating instead on a few core businesses. That concentration, combined with GE's philosophy of moving managers around as a means of developing them, made the notion of divisional long-term incentives far less attractive than it might have been at some other point in the company's evolution.

Tailoring compensation arrangements to meet the needs of a specific division can have a powerful effect, according to Gerard R. Roche, the legendary CEO recruiter and chairman of Heidrick & Struggles. "Perhaps the primary utility of differing compensation plans," he said, "is that they provide a sort of filtering process. For example, if you want to attract a risk-taker, then you can design plans that offer high risk and high reward."

A different but growing application for divisional long-term incentive plans lies in the divisions of foreign parent companies. If a person who manages a division of a Westinghouse has a hard time figuring out how he can have much impact on the results of the overall corporation, think what a hard time a person who manages a division of a Japanese parent company is going to have. Clearly, giving an executive an option on the stock of a $40 billion Japanese conglomerate isn't going to motivate him much.

Unfortunately, the stance taken by most foreign parents is to pretend that long-term incentive plans don't exist. In dealing with their U.S. executives, they try to get two forms of compensation— base salary and annual bonus—to do the work of three forms of compensation—base salary, annual bonus, and long-term incentives. But that approach usually creates more problems than it solves. Consider the experience of Burt Manning, the chairman of J. Walter Thompson, which is a subsidiary of WPP, a British advertising conglomerate. "With only two forms of compensation, you end up paying more in base salaries than you want to," Manning said. "And that, in turn, means it's harder to cut compensation costs—our key cost element in advertising—when we hit an economic downturn. So we end up having to lay off people to bring our costs in line, because cutting someone's base salary is considered taboo. And that creates yet another problem: higher severance pay costs, since severance pay tends to be a function of how much the departing employee is earning in base salary."

"With only two forms of compensation, you pay more in base salaries. That means it's harder to cut compensation costs when we hit a downturn."

Burton J. Manning
Chief Executive Officer
J. Walter Thompson

So U.S. divisions operating under foreign parents have an especially urgent need to develop long-term incentive plans that reward good divisional performance.

A final point concerning divisional long-term incentive plans involves their complexity. Compensation consultants, it seems, like to impress their clients with how much they know about finance and economics. When they design divisional long-term incentive plans, the result is often too elegant and needlessly complex. As Pfizer's Pratt says: "People simply don't understand those fancy incentive plans." After all, not all CEOs are "quants" who received their M.B.A.'s from Wharton or the University of Chicago, and those who are not probably have little patience with an overly complex incentive plan. And if senior executives don't understand those plans, as Pratt argues, then how will those plans ever motivate better performance?

Companies too often take the lazy way out in arranging compensation for their profit-center executives. One unified salary structure is a lot easier than separate, industry-focused structures for each division. Paying bonuses based on corporate performance is a lot easier than examining the performance of each division and giving the best divisions big bonuses and the worst divisions none. Granting profit-center executives options in the parent company's stock is a lot easier too, because other companies handle things that way. Besides, the company can avoid a charge to its earnings by granting stock options.

But the easy way out may not be the motivational way out. If shareholder value is going to be maximized over the long term, and if a multidivisional company has independent divisions, the design and implementation of viable divisional long-term incentive plans may give the company a significant boost toward meeting its goals.

EVERY 22 SECONDS, SOMETHING QUITE UNEVENTFUL HAPPENS SOMEWHERE IN THE WORLD.

A Citation takes off or lands safely every 22 seconds. The aircraft's safety record is even more remarkable considering there are nearly 2,000 of them in the world's largest fleet of business jets.

In aviation, the Collier Trophy is the highest tribute to excellence. The trophy was created in 1911, but 75 years went by before it was given to honor a business aircraft company.

The Citation's unmatched safety record is why that company is Cessna.

THE SENSIBLE CITATIONS

Cessna
A Textron Company

Chapter Eleven

THE NEED TO SIMULATE

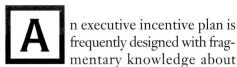n executive incentive plan is frequently designed with fragmentary knowledge about how payouts will respond to future performance. The plan designer and the CEO usually have some sort of scenario in mind. Having tested the plan under that scenario and found the response acceptable, they move on. The only problem is that since their favorite scenario is one of an almost infinite variety, it almost never comes to pass. The result: a company puts in a restricted-stock plan and gives the CEO $4 million of free shares, to be earned over the next five years simply by remaining with the company. Doubtless, the CEO and plan designer were focusing on their favorite scenario, a doubling of company stock in five years. The CEO would then take title to stock with a value of $8 million, and why not, given the magnificent appreciation? What the CEO and plan designer did not do, however, was observe that if the stock dropped by half during the next five years, the CEO would still earn $2 million in free shares.

If you are going to play the pay game fairly, it is critical to do two things. First, you must periodically simulate payouts for each of your incentive plans. And second, you must simulate payouts of your entire pay package.

For starters, take another look at the graph on page 43, which shows the relationship between a stock-option grant and a restricted-stock grant. Notice that the restricted-stock grant offers the CEO a payout even when future total shareholder return is substantially negative. Is that the sort of pay package you want under poor performance conditions? Would you be willing to print this graph in your proxy statement?

Now look more critically at this graph. Notice that until you reach the equilibrium total-shareholder-return point of about 9 percent annual growth, you are better off with the smaller restricted-stock grant. But once you pass that point, the larger stock-option grant is preferable. If you were out to maximize your income, you would doubtless like to ride the restricted-stock line when performance is less than the equilibrium point and then switch to the stock-option line when performance is above that point. In other words, you would like the best of both worlds.

Well, you can have the best of both worlds, if you persuade your board to give you a grant of stock-option shares in tandem with restricted shares. Then you won't have to guess whether the restricted stock or the options will give you the greatest future payout. No, you can wait until many years later and then, looking back, decide which grant you wish to take.

A couple of years ago, a large paper company gave its CEO a grant of 200,000 stock-option shares, in tandem with 40,000 restricted shares. The delightful results, at least for the CEO: even if the company produces severely depressed returns to shareholders—a compounded negative return of 6 percent a year over 10 years—the CEO still stands to earn $1 million from the restricted shares. If the returns to shareholders are very modestly positive—6 percent compounded, less than the 8 percent available through government bonds—the CEO will earn $4 million. And since five stock-option shares were granted for each restricted share, this CEO's payout shoots upward with a vengeance once shareholder returns increase beyond that tepid 6 percent.

Question: Would the directors have approved this plan if they had foreseen a payout so disproportionate to shareholder return? Would they have been willing to face their shareholders and defend giving the CEO a payout of $1 million for managing to depress shareholder value at the rate of 6 percent per year?

Or take another company, a gigantic airline. The CEO was given a $11.8 million restricted-stock award, but one with a twist. The company's stock was selling for about $33 per share. The restrictions on sale of the shares applied for eight years. The twist involved the board's guarantee that in the event the shares were selling for less than $33 each at the time the restrictions lapsed, the company would write the CEO a check to make up the difference. The possible results of this transaction: even if the stock price tumbled virtually to zero and dividends ceased, the CEO's restricted-stock payout would hold steady at $11.8 million.

Question: Would the board of directors have been willing to defend giving the CEO a payout of $11.8 million for heroically managing to destroy shareholder value?

Although most pay-for-performance abuses occur in the poor-performing end of the performance spectrum, occasional abuses occur in the superb-performing end as well. Take the case of a food-company CEO who was given an option grant of four million shares with a strike price of about $30 per share. Probably seeking to protect the shareholders, his board decided to cap his option gains, so that he could not make more than $125 million. Because of the grant size, however, his gains zoom to $26 million once the shareholders have enjoyed just a 2 percent return, to $57 million at 4 percent—and they peak when the shareholders earn a meager 7.4 percent, a rate that is lower than a worry-free government-bond rate.

Question: Would the directors have approved this plan if they had known it would pay the CEO $26 million for managing to increase his company's stock price by only 2 percent per year? On the other hand, wouldn't they have wondered how they were going to motivate the CEO to increase the stock price by more than about 7 percent per year?

Simulating the payout of each incentive plan helps indicate areas where the plan is unresponsive to the creation of shareholder value. Such simulations should be performed at least every three years and presented in detail to the compensation committee.

At the same time, simulate the entire CEO pay package, including base salary and incentive plans. That will help pinpoint to what extent the CEO's base salary is acting like a dead hand on the proceedings. And it will also help reveal whether the overall pay package is responsive enough to key financial indicators. You'll find out whether too much or too little emphasis is being placed on long-term performance.

Given the complexities of incentive-plan design, as well as the controversy surrounding executive pay levels, believing that you are paying for performance is no longer sufficient. You must prove you are paying for performance.

SHORTLY AFTER FLYING IN A CITATION, HUNDREDS OF PASSENGERS HAVE GONE ON TO BECOME CELEBRATED SPORTS HEROES.

In 1987 and again in 1991, hundreds of Citation owners volunteered their aircraft, pilots and fuel to airlift thousands of athletes to the International Special Olympics Games. The airlift was organized by Cessna. But the generous cooperation of Citation owners brought it to reality.

When we asked Citation owners to help these special people celebrate life in an unforgettable way, they didn't think twice.

They did it twice.

THE SENSIBLE CITATIONS

Cessna
A Textron Company

Chapter Twelve

REFORMING THE COMPENSATION COMMITTEE

I f you are a highly paid CEO, why would you want to re-form a committee willing to indulge your wildest pay fantasies? At the beginning of this book I remarked on the two hats you wear: your self-interested hat and your fiduciary hat. As this book comes to an end, permit me to appeal to your fiduciary hat.

By definition, a free market sets prices through vigorous arm's-length negotiation between informed buyers and informed sellers. There isn't much question that you are an informed seller of your talent. Not only have you been consuming your company's compensation products for years, but you are also given substantial technical help from your in-house compensation staff and your outside consultants.

But your board is not an informed buyer. We have two problems here, the first involving the "arm's-length" part of the definition of a free market, and the second involving the "informed-buyer" part. Or to put it another way, we have a single problem, a problem summarized by former Chevron CEO George Keller when he suggested, "It is justice, not mercy, that should guide a compensation committee's thinking."

A board's compensation committee is often disproportionate-ly populated by the CEOs of other companies. The reason is that they can more easily understand what executive compensation plans are supposed to do and how they work. Nevertheless, these CEOs are in an inherent conflict of interest, because whatever they do for you ends up in some database and may unwittingly provide the defense for their own raises.

Research by Charles O'Reilly of the University of California at Berkeley, Brian Main of the University of Edinburgh, and me has shown that a fairly potent predictor of a CEO's pay is the pay of the CEOs who sit on his board. In fact, knowing their pay is more helpful in predicting chief executive pay than knowing the performance of the company.

No CEO should serve on the compensation committee of a board of directors. Even a single CEO among a committee composed of five outside directors can infect the proceedings. Time after time I have seen the non-CEO members of the committee turn to a CEO member and ask, "Well, Joc, you know how these things work. Is that what we need to do?" No, I would rather populate the compensation committee with directors who have no conflict of interest. And if that means accepting people who are relatively ignorant of what goes on with executive pay, so much the better. Given that company performance can explain less than 5 percent of the variation in CEO pay, knowledge surely hasn't produced much in the way of useful results.

I do not mean to suggest that every member of the compensation committee should wear a hair shirt at each meeting. The chairman of the committee need not be a Sister of Poverty. I am suggesting only that CEOs of other companies be assigned to other board committees.

If this relatively simple change is made, more of an arm's-length stance is likely between the compensation committee and the CEO, and therefore a free market is more likely to be operating.

The second test of a free market that most compensation committees fail involves the knowledge of its members. As it now stands, the committee members cannot even remotely be considered informed buyers of CEO talent. They meet infrequently, sometimes only four times a year, and then for only one hour each time. And whatever background information they are given comes from the CEO and may not always present the full picture the committee needs to make an informed decision.

My solution is to provide the compensation committee with its own independent consultant. To provide the objectivity required, neither the consultant nor any of his associates may offer the company any other consulting services. (Lest you think I am trying to provide myself with work in my old age, I have stated publicly that I will not accept such work.) I would have the committee's consultant participate whenever it meets—in person or by phone. And I would require that the consultant's recommendations be in writing to reinforce the seriousness of the proceedings. I would also provide that the consultant's name be included in the proxy statement each year so that people like myself can study the extent to which particular consultants are associated with excessive pay or the adoption of relatively riskless forms of compensation. Finally, if the compensation committee discharges the consultant, the latter should be given the opportunity to state his case in the proxy statement. Such a privilege is now accorded a company's auditors.

Responding to the push for board reform, some companies have declared publicly that their compensation committees are free to call in the company's compensation consultants whenever they wish. But that's no reform, because the consultants continue to understand that their primary obligation is to the CEO. In the case of one company that made this declaration, the company's compensation consultant also acted as the actuary handling the pension plan of a major subsidiary. In other cases the consultant's partners may be the company's auditors.

Some other companies have declared that their compensation committees are free to call in an outside compensation consultant of their choosing, one not necessarily allied with the management. But that approach is not helpful. If the compensation committee decides to bring in an outsider, the chairman has to call up the CEO and deliver two unpleasant messages: First, our committee doesn't trust what you are telling us. And second, our committee doesn't trust what your hired gun is telling us either. Sending those messages is apt to provoke an unnecessarily defensive action from the CEO. On the other hand, if the compensation committee has its own consultant as a matter of policy, and if the consultant joins the committee every time it meets and not merely when something big is going on, the issue of trust will likely become a nonissue.

I know that some outside directors are not happy with my thinking. One compensation committee chairman told me: "If compensation committees get their own consultants, you are going to turn the whole thing into an adversarial proceeding." My response: "What do you think this is, if not an adversarial proceeding? If he is wearing his Adam Smith hat, as he should be, since he is negotiating for his own welfare, your CEO is going to try to maximize his income. And if you are wearing your fiduciary hat, as you should be while representing the interest of the shareholders, you are going to try to get him to work for as little as possible."

The fact is that boards of directors hate confrontation with the CEO. They see themselves on the same side as the CEO, not as his adversaries. And they are certainly right when it comes to the company's strategic plans and key executive promotions and dividend decisions. But in this one area of board work, the compensation committee must be the CEO's adversary to best represent the interest of the company's shareholders.

Some other outside directors have criticized my proposal on the basis of costs. One said: "We already pay a ton of money to the company's compensation consultant, and your solution is to hire a second consultant?" My response: "No law requires any company to spend a ton of money on compensation consultants. If the company wants to play the pay game fairly, it can get by with a relatively simple annual bonus plan and a relatively simple, single long-term incentive plan."

Indeed, if I could get the data, I think I could prove that there is a negative correlation between the amount a company spends on its executive compensation consultants and that company's long-term performance. Two reasons support this hypothesis: First, a compensation consultant's recommendations almost always result in someone's getting a raise, thereby increasing business costs. And second, a compensation consultant's revenues stem largely from designing add-on long-term incentive plans to shore up an incentive plan that has failed to give the CEO a huge payout and from performing extensive surveys to justify a CEO's excessive pay package. I do not mean to denigrate the contributions of an honest consultant; I mean only to indicate that at least some companies could help their shareholders by cutting back on their consultants.

Critics of CEO pay, myself included, are having a field day pointing out that no free market is operating for CEO talent. If there were, the correlation between pay and performance would be much higher. The critics look at compensation committees and see people who are friends of the CEO, who often have a vested interest in high executive pay, who spend little time studying the arcana of the company's elaborate array of incentive plans, and who, if they are willing to study the arcana, are almost never given the tutorial help they require.

If something is not done to head off the critics, it becomes a simple leap to conclude that Congress will intervene to solve the mess. Already one congressman, Sabo of Minnesota, has introduced legislation to deny companies corporate tax deductions on any pay more than 25 times that of the lowest-paid worker. And it won't be much longer before some other congressman takes note of the 1984 law imposing a 20-percentage-point surtax on excessive golden parachute pay and introduces legislation to extend that surtax to any form of CEO pay deemed excessive. A future president might even propose capping executive pay altogether—for example, by denying any executive pay of more than $1 million per year. Congress stands ready to solve problems that the free-enterprise system has been unable to solve itself. That the solutions imposed by Congress are often worse than the disease is just another reason for the business community to roll up its sleeves and solve its own problems.

If a free market for executive talent is to be preserved, shareholders, workers, and government leaders must perceive a number of things: First, that CEO pay packages are formed in the crucible of arm's-length bargaining between informed sellers and buyers of talent. Second, if CEOs in America are to receive a great deal more than their counterparts in Japan and Germany, to name but two of our key competitors, then shareholders, workers, and government leaders must perceive that U.S. companies perform better than their overseas counterparts or that American CEOs take on greater pay risk than overseas CEOs. Third, if CEOs in America are to receive huge increments of pay over their workers, once again shareholders, workers, and government leaders must perceive that CEOs' pay packages are extremely volatile. To come to this perception does not require sophisticated instruments; the observation that CEO pay plummets during national recessions ought to be sufficient.

This national dilemma of high and unresponsive CEO pay has many culprits. They include boards of directors, whose hands are usually in the open position; the Securities and Exchange Commission, which until recently has resisted requiring companies to disclose in clear language the amounts and the ways they are paying their executives; the Financial Accounting Standards Board, which for more than 40 years has been holding a sale on stock options; and compensation consultants, who have usually found it far easier to defend high executive pay than to recommend cuts for poorly performing CEOs. To this list can be added the chief executive himself, or at least the chief executive in his role of fiduciary. But it is hard to blame the CEO more than the others when the CEO, under classic economic theory, is supposed to be trying to maximize his income.

Yet you, the CEO, are going to have to solve the problem, because none of the other players have either the will or the clout. You are going to have to tell your board to take actions that permit it to bargain with you at true arm's length. You are going to have to relax the pressure placed on the SEC by your representatives, such as the Business Roundtable. You are going to have to signal the FASB that the business community will no longer block its attempts to fashion a reasonable charge to earnings for stock-option grants. And you are going to have to throw into the wastebasket the letters you get from ambulance-chasing compensation consultants who want to convince you that you are underpaid.

Some of these actions may seem against your self-interest. But they are in the interest of your shareholders, your workers, and the overall community in which you do your work. So if you think about it, they are even in your self-interest, if you insert the phrase *long term*. For you will have held at bay reformers who want to impose governmental solutions that, most of the time, make things worse, not better. And if you are seen to play the pay game fairly, and if your board of directors and its compensation committee do the same, you will have helped preserve the free-enterprise system that ultimately allows you to earn as much as you do.

Playing fair boils down to playing well. And that's to everyone's advantage, including yours.

SENSIBLE BUSINESS DECISIONS GOT YOU WHERE YOU ARE. THIS ONE TAKES YOU WHERE YOU WANT TO GO.

You've led your company through times in which others have failed. Thanks in no small part to your ability to act quickly and decisively.

But as the pace of the world quickens, you wonder if your company can continue to lead if it must follow airline schedules. For more than 1,500 businesses worldwide, the answer is no. They fly Citations.

It may surprise you to learn that a number of these companies are really not all that big. Yet.

THE SENSIBLE CITATIONS

Cessna
A Textron Company

ADDITIONAL COPIES

To order additional copies of *What Are You Worth?* for friends or colleagues, please write to The Chief Executive Press, Whittle Books, 333 Main St., Knoxville, Tenn. 37902. Please include the recipient's name, mailing address, and, where applicable, title, company name, and type of business.

For a single copy, please enclose a check for $13.95 payable to The Chief Executive Press. When ordering 10 or more books, enclose $11.95 for each; for orders of 50 or more, enclose $9.95 for each. If you wish to place an order by phone, call 800-284-1956.

Also available, at the same price, is the previous book from The Chief Executive Press, *Getting the Job Done* by Kenneth L. Adelman.

Please allow two weeks for delivery.
Tennessee residents must add 8¼ percent sales tax.